The Old Testament Always Relevant

The Old Testament Always Relevant

by ETIENNE CHARPENTIER

Translated by Sheila Richards

ST. NORBERT ABBEY PRESS
De Pere, Wisconsin
U.S.A.
1969

Excerpts from *The Jerusalem Bible,* copyright © 1966 by
Darton, Longman & Todd, Ltd. and Doubleday and Company,
Inc. Used by permission of the publishers.

Edited by Lisa McGaw

Translated by Sheila Richards

Originally published as *Jeunesse du Vieux Testament*
by Librarie Artheme Fayard.

© 1969 St. Norbert Abbey Press

Standard Book Number 8316-1036-0
Library of Congress Catalog Card Number 74-87816

Printed in the United States of America
ST. NORBERT ABBEY PRESS
De Pere, Wisconsin 54115

CONTENTS

INTRODUCTION

I was on my way back from a kibbutz where I had just spent a month, near the Egyptian border. A month fighting—alongside one hundred and fifty young people—the desert of the Negeb. The harvest was a good one: water was brought down from the north by a **sinnor** (pipeline) and another, larger one was nearing completion. When the day's work was done, people headed for the swimming pool or the lawns, where parents enjoyed a romp with their children, or to the lecture hall. Later, there was always dancing. And at 4 o'clock the very next morning, the cycle began all over again, ever new.

They were Marxists, every one of them. Their bible: Marx and Lenin.

Coming from a kibbutz, I happened across the quarter of Jerusalem where the strict sect lives. It was painful, the contrast. My Israeli friend was embarrassed. Instead of youngsters playing in the sun, naked under the arching rainbows of the gushing water, we saw little white-faced children dressed in black, stockings over their knees, weighed down with their hair dressed in locks across the temples, the remainder of the head shaven and covered in the traditional skullcap. Men in long dark coats mouthed texts from Holy Writ or lay down in the road to prevent cars being driven on the Sabbath day.

They were believers: their only book, the Holy Bible.

This might make a stranger wonder. I felt uncomfortable. For the children, perhaps; most of all, on my own account. On the kibbutz, there was life—except they were Marxists, building the kingdom upon earth; and here, they were believers awaiting the Kingdom of God, in a ghetto.

And I was a believer. Faith put me on their side. But my heart, my heart went out to the folk of the Negeb.

As a Christian, who among us has not at some stage felt the conflict between this carnal world passionately loved, and the faith for which the temporal must be renounced? Teilhard's cry from 1934 (needing to be kept in context, however) expresses it well.

> If, through some process of interior upheaval, I were to lose successively my faith in Christ, a personal God and the Spirit, I sense that I should go on believing in the World.

Again, to quote the certainty of Gabriel Marcel.

> It is my most intimate irrevocable conviction and if heretical so much the worse for orthodoxy—never mind what the saintly and wise have said—that God does not wish to be loved by us in spite of creation but glorified through the medium of creation, starting from Himself. This is what makes me find so many edifying books intolerable. This God set up against creation and in some way jealous of his own works, this to my mind is the image of an idol.

Kingdom of heaven or earth? Living history or ghetto? Christianity or Marxism?

What made me say Yes when I was asked to write this Introduction? Put simply, perhaps it was to proclaim, with the whole Bible for support, the fact that a man can love the world passionately and still be Christian; that no one can be Christian without wanting with all his might to build a better world. If the Bible had to be summed up in a sentence, it might go something like this: Because he loves it, God set the world moving in a direction which leads to an end in Christ; he is so far from despising the world he has made, that when it came to winning it back again he found nothing for it but to be made flesh.

Christianity is no ghetto. It is a people on the move to the achievement of their purpose, to give meaning to man's history: building the Kingdom of God, and this Kingdom means Someone in the end. Christianity is Christ growing to the world's end, when his mystic body will have reached the point of perfection. The Bible is the history of all this.

"Jesus Christ by himself." This is a pretty fair definition of what the Bible is all about. St. Luke says it in chapter 24 of his Gospel. You may like to read the passage over; it ranks with the finest in the whole New Testament.

Two of Christ's disciples loved him like a very dear friend. Not enough, to follow him to the Cross. When they saw him hanging there, they headed back to their own village. And Christ went after them. A pilgrim, he could have made himself known to them as he had done to others: "Yes, it is I indeed." But first he wanted to win them. They fled because the very heart of the mystery was not theirs. So he started telling them his story, out of the Old Testament. "This is what I meant when I said, while I was still with you, that everything written about me in the Law of Moses, in the Prophets and in the Psalms, has to be fulfilled. He then opened their minds to understand the scriptures" (Luke 24:38). As their love was not strong enough for them to know him in the flesh, he made himself known to them by the Scriptures. Word of God made flesh and blood, to win their hearts back to him as "Word of God in human language." In the breaking of the bread, their eyes were opened and in the eucharistic presence they knew who it was. Then they understood: his earthly life of thirty-three years followed on 2,000 years of writing about him and after it came 2,000 years of his presence in the Eucharist, the beginning of a still more mysterious presence perhaps more real and definitive, his mystic presence in his vast body which is the Church.

The scope of this book is to help you heed this Word of God, present in the past through the people of the Old Testament, who once traveled the roads of Palestine, living on now with us.

It is, then, an introduction to the Bible. Not a long-winded discussion on set topics.

To hear what someone has to say, you need first of all to be listening. One book is essential: the Bible, the Word of God in writing.[1]

You must also know the language in question and how it works. This book is intended to be of assistance to you in getting to know Bible history.[2]

But first and foremost, you need to love. I shall simply be telling you what I love about the Bible (hoping it is what matters, too!); if these few pages help one or another of you to have a heart "ready and waiting," I shall be more than glad at the outcome of my task.[3]

You may like to note one idea you can dismiss from the start.

The Bible is not one book but a whole bookshelf. The works it comprises have had to be arranged in some kind of order. Their actual order is quite empirical. Although a lot of work is being done on the composition of the Bible and some of its components, we are going to consider it from the chronological order of writing, insofar as that has been established.

For the first account of creation to come on page 1 in the Bible as we know it does not mean that it was written first. There is no doubt that it belongs to a date some four centuries later than the second account, which follows the first one. The book of Genesis in its current form is fairly recent. The books of Amos and Hosea (a thousand pages further on in your Bible) are a good deal earlier. Are you feeling a bit lost?

Right, then let's make a start.

[1]The translation of the Old Testament in the "Pléiade" series is undoubtedly the best one available in French. For preference, however, use the Jerusalem Bible in one volume. The translation is good, often very good; the main advantage lies in the notes, especially the reference system (explained on pp. xiv-xvi of the English-language Jerusalem Bible). By this means, you will be able to find out what God has to say about the big questions that concern us. The pocket edition omits the introductions and the bulk of the notes.

[2]The method of use will be set out in more detail in the latter part of Chapter 1.

[3]Editorial necessities have meant dividing this book into two volumes, this one on the Old Testament, and the second one on the New Testament. It goes without saying that they belong together.

I

GOD'S FAMILY ALBUM:
BIRTH OF A BOOK

> "Christ, here and now, for us holds the place of Omega Point, in position and in purpose."
>
> Teilhard de Chardin

1 The Future Is Behind Us . . . or, Where History Is Heading

For us, the future lies ahead, being formed out of the present, and that makes everyone stress inventing and what's new. But for the Hebrew, the past lies ahead (in Hebrew, the word means "past" and "ahead"), the past meaning the plan that God had in his heart when he made creation. History is only this plan being carried out, this primordial project we shall never really grasp, nor the angels either if it comes to that, until it is accomplished by us.

The Bible records this project and lets us know what was accomplished in the early stages; beginning and end are two great visions: (a) The beginning of Genesis: vision of the creation of the world by the Word and Spirit of God, straightway followed by the Fall. This is the human crux in a nutshell: God loves us, that is why we are here and happy; man refuses this love, he has sinned and that is why we suffer and die. (b) The end of Revelation: vision of the new creation to which we are reintroduced by the

Lamb sacrificed but living. By fighting Satan to the death, Christ fulfills this project of God's; God is not just plain God any more, but God plus, Emmanu-El or God-with-us.

God in the beginning formed this project and what we know about it (from St. Paul especially) and see already come to pass only makes the waiting harder, drawing us closer to its accomplishment ("All I can say is that I forget the past and I strain ahead for what is still to come; I am racing for the finish . . ." Phil. 3:13).

> Blessed be God the Father of our Lord Jesus Christ, who has blessed us with all the spiritual blessings of heaven in Christ.
> Before the world was made, he chose us, chose us in Christ,
> to be holy and spotless, and to live through love in his presence,
> determining that we should become his adopted sons, through Jesus Christ
> for his own kind purposes,
> to make us praise the glory of his grace,
> his free gift to us in the Beloved,
> in whom, through his blood, we gain our freedom, the forgiveness of our sins.
> Such is the richness of the grace
> which he has showered on us
> in all wisdom and insight.
> He has let us know the mystery of his purpose,
> the hidden plan he so kindly made in Christ from the beginning
> to act upon when the times had run their course to the end:
> that he would bring everything together under Christ, as head,
> everything in the heavens and everything on earth.
> Eph. 1:3-10; cf. Col. 1:15-20

This then is where history is heading: the entire universe, beings visible and invisible, of the spirit and the flesh, heading in the direction of this end point of history which is Christ; gathered up in him, we shall partake of the life of God. Dynamic vision of a universe irresistibly drawn to "all perfection" (which is Christ, see Col. 1:19); he partakes of this very perfection, since Christ was made flesh and everyone of us in him; but he also goes infinitely further, since Christ is God.

No one has communed with this dynamism of the universe like St. Paul, no one else has been able to write about it with the possible exception—though some of the terms are identical and some of the views fall short of common acceptance—of Father Teilhard de Chardin. For him, too, the universe is evolving to a point, "that dominates all cosmic evolution, constituting its crown and culmination; from this point there emanates a power of attraction which gives the entire evolutive process its inner drive and direction. This cosmic universal center of human evolution, where everything must find final union and the highest purpose, is designated in the phenomenology of the universe by the term 'Omega'" (Wildiers).

Teilhard wrote, "Now this Omega Point, as I have called it, is it not the ideal place from which to make the Christ whom we adore radiate—a Christ whose supernatural mastery is matched to our knowledge by physical power over the natural spheres of the world?" ("Christ the Evolver").

2 How God Makes History

Two visions: a project of God's love and an account of its achievement.

Between these two: the history.

But God does not run history like the operator of a

forklift truck. He runs it from the inside, coming down within the works.

That's what the Bible is: this marvelous history of God living with his people, a history of times prefiguring our own, which it contains and informs in advance.

Between sin cutting us off from the primordial vision and the consummation of God-with-us, lies a whole world! Man cut himself off from God, making himself utterly incapable of the relationship with God that was his whole life. "My son was dead," the prodigal's father will say, "and he has come back to life." For this to happen, God has to make man relearn bit by bit his childhood ways; then he can become God's child again in Christ Jesus.

The Old Testament is just the history of this tutelage, God forming the links with his people. He is going to do it by the Word. But man is so unused to listening to God that the Word in human terms takes a long time to get through, 2,000 years perhaps. When man has relearned communion, when his heart is "all on fire" to hear the Word of God, then this Word made flesh and blood will take him by the hand along the highways of the Holy Land and, fully made man, lead back to the Father the children of God that sin had scattered.

This is no place to deal with all the ins and outs of this history. You may like to have a look at the Atlas.[1] What we are going to do is to indicate the main landmarks.

1850 B.C. (perhaps 1650): **Abraham.** "Leave your country," God told this Semite whose family came from Ur. "I will give you a land and descendants." Abraham left. Abraham's faith, the start of sacred history. God speaks, Abraham goes. It is all very simple. Not a matter of law but a dialogue of love between God and his friend, in which the friend is given God's trust everlastingly.

Ca. 1250 B.C.: **Moses.** Abraham's descendants are in bondage in Egypt, symbolizing the state of degradation to which their sinfulness has reduced them.

God remembers his promise and comes to their aid, like a warrior of strong hand and outstretched arm. Through Moses he rescues the people from slavery, to bring them to his service. God remains the father leading Israel over the desert, like a man leading his children; he guides them night and day, getting angry when they let him down and punishing, but always forgiving, them.

God works at their education patiently. Because it is the time after sin, after love has been refused, the people's reaction no longer has the freedom of a little child, as in the days of Abraham, but comes under the hard taskmaster of the law on Sinai.

Ca. 1200 B.C., perhaps: Israel enters Canaan. They infiltrate through passes in the hills to the fortified townships, winning some battles: they are in the Holy Land and can proceed with the allocation.

Somewhere ca. 1000 B.C.: **The twelve tribes settle.** One link between them: the same God whose presence is in some measure made manifest by the Ark of the Covenant. This God, from whom all fatherhood takes its name, knows all about the adolescent who wants to grow up before his time. So the people say they want a king, rejecting in so doing their only King, who is God. For the moment, this is forgotten and man walks alone . . . until he calls for help when the enemy profits from his weakness to oppress him. God is always there, he comes to the rescue, raising up a savior who will free his people—for a while. The people let him down again. It is all in the book of Judges.

Ca. 1000 B.C.: **David takes Jerusalem.** Successor to the first king, Saul, David forever bears witness of what God can do when someone, even a sinful person (and what a sinner: liar, adulterer, murderer), loves Him enough to let himself be guided by Him. Solomon his son will organize the kingdom like the court of Egypt with hara and harem. This is when literature gets its start too, scribes becoming plentiful. But it is also the start of real trouble, the sin of man thinking he is big enough to make history on his own. Without God. Or—and it comes to much the same—with a good God expected to give his blessings after the deed is done, even when it is done without him or against him.

The consequences were not long in coming.

935 B.C. **The schism.** Israel now becomes two kingdoms That of the north (or Ephraim), with Samaria for capital, broke with the house of David, keepers of the promise. The kingdom of the south (or Judah) had Jerusalem for capital.

A man can be approached but he is not won over until his heart is. God goes on trying to teach the people by men whom he makes the keepers of his Word: the prophets. Sometimes speaking to the hearts of his people like a husband trying to make his wayward wife see reason, sometimes threatening, the ground is being prepared for the great purification. Israel with its kings and chariots and politics felt big enough to act alone; the lesson has to be learned, to become a little child again. God cannot act in us until our powerlessness has been accepted, and offered up: the people are going to have no power until suffering has taught them to be a people of poor men.

721 B.C.: **Samaria captured.** The kingdom of the north deported to the north of Mesopotamia by the great power of the day: Nineveh.

587 B.C. (or 586): **Jerusalem finally falls.** The kingdom of the south deported to the south of Mesopotamia, to Babylon.

587-538 B.C.: **Exile in Babylon.** The most fearful period no doubt; also the most fruitful. Suffering at last unlocks the rebel heart: "I want to go back to my father and tell him, I sinned against you."

God sends further prophets to comfort man and tell him of a new covenant.

538 B.C.: **Home from exile.** Cyrus frees the "remnant" of Israel.

From 538 to 333 B.C.: **Re-settlement difficulties. The Persian domination.** The ordinary people endure the suffering, as throughout history, for the quarrels of the great; Xerxes, Darius, the leaders; Marathon, Salamis, the battles. A time of hardship for Israel: there are no more prophets (and no one knows for how long, as the psalmist laments), no more king, an impoverished temple.

The only treasure: God's Word to the forefathers. The cult turns to meditation on the law. The wisdom books assemble the harvest of this experience.

333 B.C.: **The legendary figure of Alexander in the Middle East.** A new humanism comes in everywhere with him; at first sight, it looks irreconcilable with the law. His generals carve up the empire and this humanism is

imposed; some rule benevolently and Israel finds happiness under them (the Ptolemies of Egypt) while others are brutal (the Seleucids of Syria). When Israel comes under their yoke, from 198, the choice is once more between apostasy and death.

Beginning in the blood of martyrs, the history of the Maccabees will end in the dirt, the dynasty will produce a Herod.

In the meantime in 63 B.C., **Rome will intervene.** Under this empire in the year 6 B.C., in the middle of the night, the all-powerful Word came down from the throne of God; and a little child in the arms of the Virgin, the eternal son of God, learned of our humanity, the words for prayer to God.

Thirty years or so of age, Christ, made man and Son of God, accustoms men to living like the sons of God according to God's plan. He fulfills this in the great mystery of his death, resurrection, and ascension into heaven.

Before going from us, he leaves in the hands of his Church his presence in the Eucharist, responsible down the ages for the constitution of his mystic body.

And from Jerusalem, the Church thus poorly takes wing.

In A.D. 50, the full compass in theory is reached, insofar as founded among all peoples for whom Jews and Greeks are symbols. The apostles, meeting in Jerusalem, hold their first Council.

A.D. 70: **Fall of Jerusalem.** The distinction becomes cruelly plain, by force of Roman arms, between the Jews

so loyal to their God that they let him lead them to his
Son's Church and those still on the way. Titus takes
Jerusalem, leaving for the instant the arms of Berenice,
Herod's great-granddaughter. The temple is burned down.

The epilogue that follows is a tragic one: In 135, after
the uprising of Bar Kochba (in recent years the caves
along the shore of the Dead Sea have yielded documents
in his hand), Hadrian lets thousands of Abraham's de-
scendants-in-the-flesh be put to auction; they are banned
from setting foot in the Holy City, desecrated by the
Roman pantheon.

While waiting for those Jews sojourning along the way
to overtake us, God goes on guiding and consolidating
his people in the eucharistic body of his Son. Because his
teaching is one, the history he causes Israel to live through
remains the model for our own. In order that the unique
experience, the norm for all of ours, should not be lost,
God counseled Israel to keep a diary.

The history continues, not from the point of view of
God now but from that of the people, looking back over
their shoulders at what had happened so far.

3   Our Ever-Young Diary

> "We have only to think for a moment
> what our past has been and we readily
> perceive that though it may remain the
> same as to structural elements, the color
> of it changes and perhaps the substance
> also, in proportion as our life approaches
> the term."
>
> Gabriel Marcel, **On Looking Back**

Led by the hand of God, along goes Israel, sometimes unprotesting, sometimes protesting. But all the time, saint or sinning, there is the feeling of something extraordinary going on. "Has any god ventured to take to himself one nation" like your God? (Deut. 4:34).

Interminable discussions continue down the centuries; the people never tire of sitting under their goat-hair tents or by the waters of Egypt and telling the story of the patriarchs. Some episodes are exciting but there is more to it than that; the people somehow realize the significance of it all: their God one day, with Abraham, came into their history.

The centuries roll by. The folk-memory fragments are welded into lasting forms, and the retelling keeps the people's courage up in the dark days in Egypt. Hope is not disappointed: the living God works new marvels and for forty years the result is carried in the Wilderness wanderings. Oral tradition expands accordingly. It even covers fragments from the law, the Decalogue that Moses, perhaps, set down in writing, as the former scribe of the pharaoh of Egypt. When this material is reworked later, it becomes the basis for the books of Genesis and Exodus, and for part of Numbers.

Now it is the turn of the judges. Just as a boy is never done telling his pals what he has been up to, so Israel had an unfailing fund in the stories concerning the saviors. Besides, the knowledge of writing was at the stage that this or that piece from the life of Samuel or Saul could be jotted down; the story of the holy king, David, could be relived, the Song of the Bow transcribed for children at school to learn, the lament of David for Jonathan preserved (2 Sam. 1:17-27).

The court of Solomon had its scribes, the royal chronicles were kept properly up to date. But if an adolescent likes hearing history, he also likes to dream of the past. He loves wonder stories he invents for himself about the origin of himself and of the world, about creation. He does not actually know what happened but he knows God loved him and that is why he exists, that he failed this love and that is why he is miserable.

From this time onward he keeps in his album a record of all the words that are momentous to him, the spiritual experiences brought him by the extraordinary men who were bearers of the Word of God just as one would enter the confidences of a friend, a priest: they may have made us feel at a loss but we became better people because of them.

In about 750 B.C., the first of these prophets—Hosea—revealed to the people that God's love was like the love of a young man for his future bride. That message gave life a new dimension. Everyone put himself in the place of the bride-to-be, when the bad days in the desert unsustained except by this love were like a long engagement; and in the diary, infidelity turns to adultery and prostitution, the response to God using the language of love.

For some while, this young man collects—so that he can repeat them—his prayers, his songs of joy and those of pain, his cries of suffering, his anguish and his aspirations. The book of Psalms draws on the religious experience of all the ages.

But the testing time has come, when life is hard. He did not believe the prophets when they foretold it would come to pass. Now exile has brought his false hopes and

illusions tumbling down, with all its sufferings, wretchedness, death and destruction; he has to start thinking from
the beginning again. The one reality left to him gradually
becomes plain: God.

All the time, his album is getting more full, whatever
else happens. In exile, among a people with many divin-
ities and set cult ways, he reflects on what is special
about his religion: he gets to know better what sets his
own people apart, separate, holy and "holy because their
God is holy." The book of Leviticus develops this theme,
in the wake of the prophet Ezekiel.

The exile comes to an end. They all troop home to
Palestine, their only treasure in the faith and the texts
that have accrued down the ages. It is the time of wisdom.
Man matured by experience finds himself alone, face to
face with essentials. Israel expresses its experience or
the serious problems it confronts, now in the worldly wise
passages of Qoheleth, now lyrical as in Job. Above all,
the moment has come to look through the old records.
Concerning the history of the patriarchs and the Wilderness, a priest assembles at least four traditions, composed
over periods of time. Amalgamated through his efforts
into a harmonious synthesis, these five books, the Pentateuch, become the law of the people of God.

About this period (ca. 400 or 300 B.C.), a look back
over what has gone before and a gathering up of all the
documents written by such a variety of men during the
people's existence—like turning the pages of a snapshot
album—gradually gives the astonished people a sense of
the direction of their lives. All these events, apparently so
disparate, meant one thing. Someone was leading them.
In discovering God in their everyday lives, the people

found—with the force of a revelation—that all the pointers, the human fragments, written by men who were very mortal, all added up to one book! An inspired book, because, whatever the passage of the text, Someone is speaking there.

Every book, every episode in the history falls into place with the revelation of God's plan as the people begin to glimpse it, just as each piece of a jigsaw puzzle goes to make up the final picture.

Israel discovers its book.

And bit by bit, the people begin to wonder whether the Word therein expressed, which made them and led them, is not something more than a simple word; it is the Word that shares the throne of God, it is the image of God invisible, reflecting the substance thereof; the very same that went through the world looking for an abiding place, to whom God said, ". . . make your inheritance" (Sir. 24:8). "The Word was made flesh, he lived among us" (John 1:14).

Wonderment of the apostles, the first Christians. They knew the Word by heart in its literary existence. It was given to them to see and to touch. The care they took in transmitting it to us is very understandable. Embarking with the whole Bible on a history the ending of which is the constitution of Christ in totality, the incarnate Word, they were aware that down the ages the driving force behind progress to this end would be that same Word. The Church's veneration for the text is very understandable, in that God lives through it; the Church knows that it was created by the Word and continues to be so unceasing, and that it is responsible for transmitting the Word to mankind by reading it to the people: for the Word is without possible error since it is the Word of

God himself. But the Church also knows that in the end only the Church can understand its real meaning because it enshrines the Holy Spirit that inspired the book.

The Church, which is to say ourselves, you and me, may God grant we are obedient to his Word, the light upon our path and the driving force of our lives: for the Church acts as companion to us upon our path, drawing us irresistibly to itself which is Omega Point.

—   —   —   —   —   —

In this chapter, an attempt has been made to convey without too much burden of detail some basic notions for a Christian reading of the Bible.

It may be useful to summarize them in a more concrete form and perhaps more concisely. (This summary may be omitted now if the reader wishes, and returned to later.)

Bible and theology. The Bible is not a catechism but God's family album.

To get to know someone, I can set about studying his anthropometric form, classify him according to the characteral system of Le Senne, find out his genealogy. I shall know all about him then except perhaps that he is a man and I can love him! If I spend an hour with his little boy leafing through the family album, I may come away not knowing his actual height but I shall know a bit about his heart.

The role of theology, of catechism: to give me exact notions about God. The Bible is a family album. The heart of God beats all through it.

Biblical theology. It aims to systematize what God tells us about himself in the pages of the album.

Foundation of this branch of learning: the belief that the seventy-three books of the Bible are one book.

Seventy-three books grouped piecemeal on the bookshelf, their composition covering a span of one thousand years. Hundreds of authors had a hand in it, of different mentalities and different languages (Hebrew, Aramaic, Greek). The subjects have nothing in common. Ridiculous to try and have one list of contents for the sake of studying cross-references!

Beyond the profound human diversity, there lurks a profound unity: the Bible is one big book because the same Spirit inspires all the authors, because the same Word of God is expressed throughout.

This explains the mysterious cross-references that occur from one end of the book to the other, especially between the Old Testament and the New. We have mentioned the two visions that make up the frame. We shall be dealing with others when discoursing on topics.

The Bible can therefore be read in two ways. In horizontal layers, by books: as in a cathedral one stops before this door, that sculpture, this glass, giving each its due according to the history of art; or in vertical lines, according to the book: on this analogy, I find myself standing at a keypoint where I can see all the detail in an over-all view and thus commune with the dynamism informing the whole monument.

Inspiration. The fact that the Bible has two authors: God (or rather, God through the Holy Spirit), and man.

It is a mystery, that is sure. But only one aspect of the mystery of God's action in the world, of the freedom and grace of every one of us. J. M. Aubert gives a good example in illustration of this point in his volume in the "Jalons" series:[2] Scientific research and Christian faith; this divine action "far from harming that of created beings, far even from juxtaposing itself with the same, constitutes it in its own order, reaches it within, sustains it in its existence but leaves it its specific nature" (Aubert, p. 90).

But is man aware of this? Not necessarily and probably not habitually. I am not aware at every moment of the day that God sustains my existence and has made me do what I do. However, God does sustain me all the days of my life and forever, even when I use the vitality the wrong way and sin; but God takes charge of the man he inspires only within time limits, and in such a way that this man cannot commit errors (privilege of inerrancy).

Two good analogies crop up from time to time to illustrate inspiration: God, author of the Bible (take heed, the temptation is to forget that man is also the author of it); man, instrument of God. (So is my pen! You see how careful you need to be not to get caught out, it being neither intelligent nor free.)

What is inspired in the Bible? All of it, obviously.

When I act, all my acts are performed under the moving power of God. When the inspired man writes, he is likewise under the moving power of God, who takes him over just as he is, with his temperament and learning, passions and limitations—and **everything** he writes is inspired.

Who is inspired? The Bible, the Book the Church puts into my hands is inspired: thus all those who collaborated intelligently in its composition were inspired. (It matters little that the discovery has recently been made that the second part of the book of Isaiah is not Isaiah's. The whole book called Isaiah is inspired, so therefore is the author of the second part.)

Inerrancy. There are no errors taught in the Bible.

That much is plain: if it is the Word of God, it cannot be deceiving.

And yet errors abound? (The creation in six days, light created before the stars.) True. And as the boundaries of knowledge advance (from geology to history), no doubt more errors will be discovered. But the learned astronomer who says to his son, "The sun is rising"—is he in error? He talks as everyone does, to be understood. The problem would be different if he used the expression at a learned meeting. The Bible talks everyday language. So it commits "errors." But it does not teach errors. In other words, in each instance the question must be asked: What is the author trying to say? in order to establish what measure of credence he is giving (and wishes to have us give) to what he has to say. For that, the literary genre he is using needs to be discerned.

Literary genres. The form selected by the writer to convey his thought.

It is as Pius XII recalled, the key to the interpretation of the Bible. The truth of a historical novel is not the same as that of a historical book; if it evokes the environment, even if the details are incorrect, then it is true. The choice of genre is governed by the intention of the author: to amuse, to instruct, to give comfort, and it indicates to the reader the way in which the writer wishes to be read and believed. A contribution for a humorous magazine and Lalande's dictionary of philosophy do not look or read the same.

All the literary genres of ancient times in the Middle East occur in the Bible. Discerning which is which is one of the nicest tasks the commentor has to face and the biggest one in respect of the result of interpretation. The nonspecialist must trust the specialist in this domain in most instances.

Meaning of what is written. There is only one, the literal meaning. That is, in each text the author wants to tell us something and it comes across from the words he uses.

The difficulty is that the author here is two, God and man!

That which the human author is trying to tell me with the words he uses we call the first or immediate literal meaning.

The divine author, using the same words, may on occasion wish to say more than the inspired man could comprehend. In this instance, we speak of the second or plenary literal meaning.

This plenary meaning, which thus exceeds the human author, will not become intelligible to us until the threshold which is Christ has been crossed. It is only in him that what is written finds full meaning. To give an example:

In 740 B.C. Isaiah told King Ahaz that a boy would be born and his name would be "Emmanu-El" or "God-with-us." Whether Isaiah had in mind little Hezekiah or the future Messiah, he can only have been thinking of a man by whom God would make himself present with his people as never before. In this expression, the Spirit already discerns the figure of the Son of God made man. When Matthew applies the name to Jesus (Matt. 1:23), he is only making explicit this plenary meaning. The same expression, Emmanu-El, therefore has twice-deep meaning, immediate or plenary but always literal.

This plenary meaning will be dubbed "typical meaning" when the twice-deep sense affects not a notion but a being: Isaac is the "type" of Christ going up to Calvary. The crossing of the Red Sea, the "type" of baptism.

Canonicity. The fact of being inscribed on the canon (catalogue) of holy books.

The seventy-three books of the Bible, and they alone, are canonical.

Texts. Some names currently used:

Hebrew: often called the Masoretic text (from the name given the Jewish scholars who vocalized the written text from the seventh century A.D.).

Greek of the Old Testament: the Septuagint (referring to the version of the seventy men who, according to tradition, translated the Hebrew text; see below, p. 186, n. 3).

Latin: Vulgate (**editio vulgata,** the Latin edition as revised by St. Jerome).

— — — — — —

In respect of method of use.

You will have already gathered that in this book we are going to "do" the whole cathedral, stopping at each door and window, but only to get the general idea and its relevance to the whole, in order to appreciate the dynamism in totality and to make you want to take a closer look at it.

In other words, these pages are going to give as it were a literary history of the Bible. You will be invited to read the books in the (probable) order in which they saw the light; I shall try to show for each of them how the authors stand in regard to their times and how they influenced their times.

The material will be considered in three main divisions: (1) Books of the Old Testament, the time of preparation—which is the substance of the present volume. (2) Books of the New Testament, the time of realization of God's plan in his Son and through the Church. (3) Revelation: the vision of the time of achievement in the celestial city. Sections 2 and 3 listed here (New Testament and Revelation) will be dealt with in a second volume.

[1] A historical atlas will be very handy. An excellent one within the reach of all pockets is Father Luc Grollenberg, *Shorter Atlas of the Bible,* trans. Mary F. Hedlund (New York: Nelson, 1959).

[2] Reference is to Jalons (Landmarks) series *Je Sais . . . Je Crois* published in France; *The Old Testament—Always Relevant* is one of the Jalons series books.

II

ARRIVAL OF THE PEOPLE:
FROM ABRAHAM TO
THE PROMISED LAND

At the beginning of the second millennium B.C. the whole Middle East gives the impression of a ferment, like a stream of molten lava, of formidable dimensions, formidable not so much for the suddenness of irruptions but because of the inexorable momentum amassing along its course.[1] Semitic tribes go up out of the desert of Arabia or come down from the plateaus of Iran: as one wave impels another, so they drive out other tribes before them. Ur falls. A new dynasty comes to power in Babylon. The Hittites settle in Anatolia and the Hurrites in Mesopotamia. The onrush advances in waves that crisscross as ground is gained here and a repulse administered there. As the tide reaches the family group, unhurriedly they get together, pack their tents, herd the stock, and set out to displace some other family group in new quarters. In 1730 B.C., the tide reached Egypt. The period from 2000 to 1785 B.C. was one of splendor (Middle Theban empire, 11th and 12th dynasties, with the Amenemat and Sesostris). But the invaders—the Hyksos or shepherd kings—arrive to settle in the delta. For two hundred years, the Semites remain masters.

> **"God of Abraham, Isaac and Jacob,**
> **not the philosophers and sages . . ."**

Just as the spotlight from a projector casts a pool of

brightness in a theater filled with shadows, so the divine light picked out one family group from all others in the great and nameless stream of moving lava; it was about the year 1850 B.C. (perhaps 1650). They had come from Ur and stopped at Haran, uprooting themselves like all the other families because they had to. Abraham meant to lead a quiet life here on earth like his father before him, no different from anyone else—that is how it goes with all such lives. He was not then aware that God had made friends with him and that he was to become father of all those to be born by his faith.

"God said to Abraham . . ." That is how the story always begins. God utters and his Word makes what is said come to pass. Eight or nine hundred years later, the same thought was in the mind of the writer of the creation story. "In the beginning . . . God said, Let there be light, and there was light."

"Leave your country . . ." To every life, the Word of God offers a new break from the past with its shibboleths and security.

"Go to the land I will give you . . ." It is going to be his indeed, providing he receives it as God's gift.

And Abraham goes. It is that simple. Faith is simple. It does not mean having to know endless numbers of things about God first (what is that to Abraham?); when God says go, he goes. Faith moves the whole being of the person given over to God, betting his life on it.

The molten lava moves slowly and hope goes with it, as the family group move to a land they do not know.

In Canaan, God makes a formal covenant with his

friend. Covenant? More of a promise, since God alone is the committed party to the undertaking. In an extraordinary ceremony, described in Genesis 15, God agrees to be "cut in half" like the sacrificial animals if he fails to honor his promise. His promise has no strings attached. Once and for all, God has undertaken to lead man to well-being in the land and people of God. However great our sins may be, God cannot utter a disclaimer. The strange bargaining of Gen. 18 witnesses the arrangement when Abraham wears himself out asking God for forgiveness. Abraham left everything—and his security, his only security henceforth (and our own), is trust in God.

The step is essential to anyone who turns to God in Faith, and must be perfect and complete from the first instant or not at all. But to keep it up, a constant process of adjustment to God's plan makes it plainer, the more the dialogue serves to indicate what is required.

God said to Abraham, "I will make you a great nation." But his wife was childless. God told him what would happen. He did not say how. Man must do the finding out. God sees to everything, on condition we do our utmost. It was a struggle for Abraham, endeavoring with might and main to carry out God's plan. One each occasion God made fresh demands and caused Abraham to improve his performance still further to the point of total commitment.

> Gen. 12: departure for an unknown destination, on the vague promise of fathering a great people. His wife childless.
> Gen. 15: to arrange matters, Abraham decides to adopt one of his household. God says, No . . . of your own flesh and blood.
> Gen. 16-17: as the custom was in the circumstances,

Abraham went to one of his slave girls: birth of a son, Ishmael. God says, No . . . of your wife who has borne no child.

Gen. 22: God is the one who quickens the dead. By his wife Sarah, Abraham has a son, Isaac. God then says, Sacrifice to me your son.

God is a father too and knows the pain of seeing his son die on the wood. God knows then that Abraham loves him.

Saint Abraham. Friend of God and father of all believers.

Thus, in the morning of our history, all has been said. In the history of the world as in that of each one of us, we see how God moves and how we ought to answer in faith. (For further reading: Gen. 12-50.)[2]

Some tales of Isaac, Jacob, and Joseph. Then silence for four hundred years; God's voice is still.

Toward 1300 B.C., the spotlight comes on again and shows a raggle-taggle of slaves in a little province of Egypt making bricks for the pharaoh's building schemes, under the eye of the slavedrivers.

What has happened? The Hebrews, part of the moving tide, with the Hyksos or without them, went down to Egypt. Protected by these Semites, they were enabled to settle and to prosper in the land of Goshen. The Hyksos were expelled. And they stayed on, suspect to begin with and soon persecuted.

The children of Abraham cry then to God. And God remembers their father Abraham and the covenant.

With Abraham, God himself intervened because it was the beginning of sacred history, also because Abraham and he were friends.

Now his new way of getting things done makes a first appearance, always to be used from that time on; namely, through individuals. His choice falls on Moses.

For a start, God makes him break with the past (Exod. 2) and sends him off into the desert. Then—looking to the future, when God wants a man for important work on behalf of his people—he is shown a little of the sphere of God. Exodus 3 and 4 give the story of how Moses was called. Love, one of the great features the Bible should reimpart to readers, has two component parts. One is respect and the other intimacy. If one is missing, there is not love but fear (attitude of a wife to her lord and master in some civilizations), or possession (a man possesses a daughter). In the presence of God, the Wholly Other, Moses can only bow down in respect and adoration. He is going to become more intimate with God than any other man.

God gives Moses his name, meaning in Semitic language that he gives of himself, since the name partakes of the essence to some extent. "To say someone's name summons that person's presence, operative in a way that is as immediate as inevitable" (Auzou).

Note on the names of God:

God is sometimes called "El" (or in the plural, denoting majesty, "Elohim"). A common name, El becomes the proper name for the divinity among the Semites. (Also found in Allah, a contraction of "The God," Al-Illah.) Many given names derive from it: Gabri-El, "God is strong"; Rapha-El, "God heals"; Mica-El, "Who is like God?"; Elisabeth, "She promises by God"; Emmanu-El, "God with us."

But God is unknowable. So man cannot know his name. This is why those who love God call him,

"God of Abraham," "God of the Lord Jesus Christ."

Twice, God seems to have been defined.

First, to Moses, being defined as the undefinable: "I am Yahweh." Scholars are not agreed on the exact sense of this word. From the root "to be" or rather "to be doing," the name is less a definition than a pointer; "it leaves intact, total, the mystery of God. But it makes the mystery an immediate neighbor, impressive and wonder-working" (Auzou). When he says the name (**Adiutorium nostrum in nomine domini,** "Our help is in the name of Yahweh"), the believer, Israelite or Christian, brings God near and acting for him. Lastly, the sense comes not from philology but history: our God is Yahweh-who-brought-us-out-of-the-house-of-Egypt, who works in our history. The full perfection of the name will not be definitively known until Jesus, short for Yoshuah, "Yahweh saves."

Communication of the name of Yahweh taught us he was "savior." A second revelation will show why, because he is "love." Revelation to Moses again, but after the people sinned, scorning the covenant of God at the very time he was dictating the terms to Moses on Mount Sinai (the golden calf episode, see Exod. 32-34). The first occasion God stood for "giving"; after sin, he became "for-giving," something more.

In Exod. 34:6-7, he gives, as Father Gelin nicely says, his calling card. "Yahweh, a God of tenderness and compassion . . . . rich in kindness and faithfulness." Each term is rich in contextual history. "Tenderness from the root that means the mother's breast; God who makes mothers has, like them, kindness "every morning . . . renewed" (Lam. 3:23). "Compassion," the image best conveying the root word, is that of the mother lovingly leaning over her little child (cf. Je-an short for Yo-hanan, 'God makes grace'). "Rich in kindness" (the word that overwhelmed Hosea), the image that of the tenderness of an engaged couple. "Faithfulness," our "Amen" is from the same root and expresses the security of the person who knows he can rely on the one solid reality.

This note on the names of God has carried us a bit far forward in the history. We come back to the "definition in deed" of Yahweh, in the crossing of the Red Sea. This has received a good deal of publicity recently (more's the pity[3]) in the film version of the **Ten Commandments,** so the text presents no difficulties except it proves too much! The miracle is actually a hindrance. A little more needs to be said on the subject.

Note on biblical miracles:

That God can work miracles is on record. He worked a great many, however, that he did not deem useful for us to have on record (see St. John's explicit statement about Christ's miracles, John 20:30).

When dealing with a miracle story, the first question to ask is not "How, where, and when did it happen?" but "Why has the fact been recorded?" Put another way, "What does the author—God and man—want to tell me by it?" Remember, it is the key to interpretation of the Scriptures, enabling us especially to know exactly wherein God engages his truthfulness by privilege of inerrancy in the Bible (in this realm, often best left to the experts).

Sometimes God wants to teach the materiality of the miracle, e.g., the bread of the Last Supper become the body of Christ.

It is not impossible that other times God wants only to leave us with a record of his miraculous passage in history. Then he leaves to the recorder some freedom of choice of media (the literary genre) most apt to convey this passage of his.

For example, the crossing of the Red Sea. Studying the literary genre of this episode, the experts tend to conclude that the author does not want to teach us the materiality of the fact (of the wall of spurting water in the film, let me just say: it was not like that!); the author wants to tell us that God intervened in a miraculous way. The people, in human terms, were done for; God saved them; and to do it he used water, water meaning salvation for him and death for his foes.

Likewise, the story of the theophany (manifestation of God's presence) on Mount Sinai. The text is clear, God intervened in the life of his people, uttering and making a covenant with them. The fulgurating passage of God marked the heart of Israel with fear (meaning respectful love) of this God, a devouring fire. All this the inspired author wishes to convey to us. That is what is inspired and inerrant. As to the literary expression with which the people clothed their impression touching God who speaks, I must examine it with care. It is possible God took advantage of a great mountain storm to make the people aware of his presence (as he did with the natural phenomena of the Nile tides, the reddening of the water, and the locusts). It is also permissible to hold that God made himself manifest (how? one does not know) and that this description of the manifestation, this theophany, "may owe certain features to the two most majestic spectacles vouchsafed to mankind: a sub-tropical thunder-storm and a volcanic eruption."[4]

By the miracle of the Red Sea, God makes of this motley band of onetime slaves a People on the march together to a single end, the Promised Land, under a single leader, Moses.

God had only to make them his people by the covenant on Sinai. (For further reading, Exod. 19-24.)

As distinct from the covenant with Abraham—a promise, a unilateral pact—the covenant with Moses (not detracting from the promise to Abraham one whit) is a bilateral contract (cf. the expressive rite in Exod. 24:8 and note). God undertakes, as he had done with Abraham, to lead the people to well-being, but "on condition that . . ." This modifies the relation of the people with him. Since the time of Abraham, God, to be a just God, has to guide the people to well-being, whether they are sinners or not. He has promised and his justice is faithfulness. The promise is not set aside; yet, from the time of Sinai, God, to be just, will have to observe the terms of contract and in so doing refuse well-being to a sinning people; his justice becomes vindicatory.

This apparent contradiction underlies the whole of the Old Testament (and the life of every one of us) and will only be resolved in Christ upon the cross.

It is sometimes said that God forgets our sins; because he is merciful, he forgives them without exacting penance. This is not true and my whole dignity as a man is called in question by this pretended present. I made a contract with God; I have broken it. If God believes in the dignity of man and thus in a contract made with him, then he ought to respect it and punish if need be. For God, a contract made with man is not like a children's game where one can cry, "Pax! I am not playing any longer." It was neecssary, St. Luke says several times, that Christ should suffer. Therein lies the treasure of God's love. He is just and therefore has to let man die; but he is also just in the sense of faithful and must come to the rescue. He will be supplying the victim; in God's Son, all mankind dies to sin; and in him, all mankind—that is, you and I—attain well-being.

This dialectic of love, fully respecting man, is already touched on in the episode of the golden calf; at the very time God is announcing his covenant, the people are sinning. God then reveals himself forgiving. (Read Exod. 32-34.)

After that, it is life in the Wilderness. The purifying march strewn with failures and the forty-year sojourn (the Semite way of saying, for the space of one generation) at Kadesh where Moses organizes the people of God. (Read Num. 11-14.)

One towering figure throughout this story is that of Moses. One word describes him: responsible. A man apart, responsible on behalf of God to the people and on behalf of the people to God.

Moses is on the side of God, who chose him as mediator in the two events creating a People out of a disorganized group, namely, delivery from Egypt and the covenant on Sinai (Exod. 14; Deut. 5:1-5; Exod. 20:19-21, 24; 33:7-11). He is the faithful servant who works wonders, never forgetting that he is the servant and no more. His characteristic attitude of mind, according to the Bible, was humbleness, or better still, he was "poor," "small," and "abandoned" in the hands of God (Num. 12:3). How tempting it is when God trusts us with a responsibility to make it "our" affair. Moses escaped this danger, no doubt because of his unique intimacy with God (see Exod. 33:11-23). Indeed, Jewish tradition treats him tenderly, misreading Deut. 34:5: he died from a "kiss of God."

Moses is on the side of men, of the people to whom he belongs—this side of sinning—and to whom he feels tied. When God permits him to enter into the greatest intimacy ever, his one plea is: "Forget not your people" (Exod. 34:9). He must suffer on behalf of the people (Deut. 9:18) and because of them (Num. 20:12; Deut. 3:23-28). Above all, he feels responsible for the people when he has to take their part even against God himself. God will one day go so far as to propose destroying the people and starting again with Moses himself, as formerly he had started with Abraham. Moses will answer, "Kill me rather than lead me to well-being without my people." (One hesitates to transpose this into Christian terms but it would go something like this: "I would rather be damned than find myself in heaven without those for whom I am responsible.") See Exod. 5:22-23; 32:7-14, 30-32; Num. 11:10-15; 14:10-19.

Moses is the figure of the "suffering servant" in Isaiah and, moreover, of Christ upon the cross torn between the Godhead which he is and the man he has become, "made sinful for our sakes." He is the figure, also, for every Christian who, in Christ, knows himself responsible for his brethren.

Note on the Composition of the Pentateuch:

Of the life of Christ we have four accounts, those of Matthew, Mark, Luke, and John. Four accounts, the publication of which spread over some thirty or forty years. There have always been attempts to weld them into a whole, a single account of the life of Jesus (the four Gospels in one only).

What the Bible did not want to happen with the life of Jesus has happened with the life of God's people from Abraham to the land of Palestine. What is called the Pentateuch (Genesis, Exodus, Leviticus, Numbers, and Deuteronomy—perhaps Joshua in addition) is really a four-in-one account, four accounts in composition ranging over twelve or thirteen centuries and allowing some five hundred years for writing them down. First told in the tents and transmitted by oral tradition, these accounts were written down at different dates. The first tradition (called Yahwist, known by the letter J because it calls God Jahweh, or Yahweh) no doubt from Solomon in the southern kingdom (ca. 950?); the second (Elohist, known as E, calling God Elohim), in close parallel a little later (ca. 850?) in the northern kingdom; the third (Deuteronomic, D) has a lot of affinity with the northern prophet Hosea (ca. 750); and last, the Priestly tradition (P, of the Priestly Code) is later, from the time in exile and under the influence of the prophet Ezekiel. It goes over all this history to get a theological synthesis.

Harmonizing these four accounts in one may have been done after the exile, between 500 and 300 B.C.

For more detail, see the Introduction to the Pentateuch in the Jerusalem Bible. A labor that will take a bit longer but pay dividends is to mark the different traditions in the margins of our Bible, using the notes and different-colored pencils.

As we decided to proceed as far as possible in sequence of composition, the difficulty we are in can be envisaged.

To simplify things and avoid doing the same history four times over, in this chapter and the next I am relying on the older traditions, J and E; later, we shall be seeing how tradition D and in particular P re-read this history to get at the depth of meaning. The traditions, it must not be forgotten, were oral; that is, they were in existence prior to being recorded.

[1]See the map in the map section at the back of the Jerusalem Bible.

[2]Some bits may shock us in their reality. It must not be forgotten the Bible is no smooth history but first and foremost God's family album, and the family were rough diamonds at the outset. For the literary aspect, see the end of this chapter where there is a note on the composition of the Pentateuch.

[3]A good documentary of life in Egypt, but it takes no account

of the Bible's religious meaning. The shell has been taken for the substance, the literary genre for the message.

The first-rate short-length puppet feature about the life of Moses, on the contrary, constantly takes us beyond what is expressed, to approach the Word of God.

[4]W. F. Albright, *From the Stone Age to Christianity* (Baltimore: Johns Hopkins Press, 1940), p. 200.

III.

THE KINGDOM:
A PEOPLE IN SEARCH
OF MATURITY

1 **When God Turns Historian** (Joshua, Judges, Samuel, Kings)

There are no historical books in the Bible. I hear you protest: The Bible is called sacred history and what about all the stories concerning the conquest of Palestine, David and Goliath, Samson—isn't that history? I understand the objection and, instinctively, would classify the whole under the heading of historical books (as modern editions of the Bible usually do). But there is nothing I can do; consult the table of contents as Christ read it (Luke 24:46) and as the Jews still do (see "The Hebrew Bible" in the Jerusalem Bible, p. xii). The Old Testament comprises three parts: the Law (yes, of course; all the stories concerning the exodus and Moses, that is what the law is); the Prophets; and the Writings, meaning to say the remainder (some say the Psalms, as being the best-known book). No trace at all of historical books.

We enter on a new category, that of the prophetic books, with the four titles to be dealt with now: Joshua, Judges, Samuel (2 books) and Kings (2 books). They tell the history of the people from arrival in Palestine (ca. 1250 B.C.) to the end of the southern kingdom (587 B.C.). They are called the earlier prophets, to distinguish them from the later ones we shall be meeting in the next chapter.

Had they not seen the day after the "binding" of this second part of the Bible, the following would also be included: the two books of Chronicles (history from Adam down to 587); Ezra and Nehemiah's recollections (from ca. 538 to ca. 400) and the books of the Maccabees.

Paradox: these prophetic books which are not historical concern history, that is to say, the past, whereas a prophet foretells the future!

Here we come no doubt to the heart of the problem. For the Bible, a book of history does not tell only of the past, and a prophet does not foretell the future.

At this point and at the risk of anticipating, it is no doubt useful to consider what a prophet is.

PROPHETS

Read first the stories of the calling of Isaiah, Jeremiah, and Amos. Re-read that of the calling of Moses (Isa. 5; Jer. 1; Amos 3:3-8; Exod. 3; 33:18-23).

Starting from their experience, let us try and see what a prophet is (also, in what sense the twentieth-century Christian ought to be one).

● The prophet is a man who has "seen" God.

This vision is not necessarily something extraordinary from which the average Christian who has "seen" Christ only through the Gospel is cut off altogether. See Jeremiah; before he was called, he was already leading a life of obedience to and intimacy with God. The moment of his calling comes when this communion with God "takes such a constraining aspect that, under the form of vision, it imposes itself like a new reality" (E. Jacob). The same holds for Hosea and Amos. No doubt for Isaiah too.

What does he see? Not what God is. He is the unknowable; but what God does in his plan of love for the world.

Thus, for instance, the Bible nowhere tells us that God is a trinity (one God in three persons), but speaks of the Father who loves us, the Son who comes looking for us to lead us to his Father, and the Spirit filling our hearts.

In revealing his mysterious plan for loving us, God draws us into intimacy with him. That is what the prophet is called to, the knowledge of this mystery.

● The prophet is a man who, having entered into the plan of God, sees everything with the eyes of God.

For the prophet, from then on everything speaks of God, everything is a sign. Jeremiah may be looking at a branch of almond ("watcher" in Hebrew); it makes him think of God, who watches over him. Jesus sees the flowers of the field and in the flowers he sees the love of God the Father.

(Is everything a sign from God for me, does the whole world speak to me of him: events, family, pleasures and displeasures, work, others?)

● The prophet is a man from then on responsible for the Word of God.

Of this Word of God, the concrete expression of God's loving plan (soon to be incarnate) which comes to men in words and deeds but henceforth always through the mediation of other men: God wants to need men.

This Word expressed in human words, the prophet must bring to men.

(Every Christian is still the bearer of this Word, this good news which is Jesus in the Gospel, which is the eucharistic Christ living in each of us as in his temple. Is the Christian not responsible for bearing this Word to others, as it transforms his life and is the secret of his joy?)

This Word, expressed in human events, is what the prophet must reveal to men. Because he has entered into the plan of God, he sees everything with the eyes of God, he makes others see God in everything. The Israelites were apparently living a profane history like all other histories. The prophet by his preaching and his life, makes them see God in it, discovering the mysterious side of their lives. He transforms their history into sacred history.

(Does my life make problems for those with whom I live? Does it make them think that God lives in them too, that their lowly daily round is a sacred history?)

● A man who is a prophet is so because God has chosen him, and not because of his intelligence, boldness, or some other characteristic.

Compare the temperaments of these men; God takes them on as they are, the good qualities along with the bad: Isaiah, the aristocrat, politically adept and decisive; Jeremiah, the villager with the sensitive soul made for the life of home; Amos, the laborer who calls a spade a spade and the great ladies of Samaria "cows"; Ezekiel, the eccentric who can never do or say anything the same as everyone else.

> You did not choose me,
> no, I chose you;
> and I commissioned you
> to go out and to bear fruit,
> fruit that will last; . . .
> John 15:16

Earlier prophets

This portrait of the prophet applies in the first instance to the men of genius who, from the seventh century, are going to change the face of Israel.

Perhaps you are beginning to understand that preferring the title of prophetic to historical (together with the Bible) means more than passing fancy since it affects their interpretation. Suppose someone hands you a bar of steel and asks you to study it, what you say will be affected by whether the result is an essay on industrial design or molecular physics; in other words, according to the literary genre, which has been set you. Now, to take a closer example: over a certain period of time, you may collect documents for making a history or attempt a philosophy of history.

"Prophetic books": the title tells me that the author in narrating the past is not primarily concerned—never mind appearances—with secular history, but first and foremost with furthering God's plan enacted through this history. These books teach us to read, in the events of the life of Israel—and by contrast in our own—the Word of God addressed to us. The bar of steel looks solid, calm, rectilinear, and problem-free: I need an expert's help to perceive the life of the material in movement, its dynamism and potential energy to be released. The main benefit from reading these books: to make us perceive in the life of Israel and our own, beyond the commonplace appearance, the dynamism of the Word of God drawing us toward the final end of history. "The Word is very near to you, it is in your mouth and in your heart for your observance" (Deut. 30:14).

This no doubt was little appreciated at the time the

events occurred and were first given form, either orally or in writing (very soon after the events themselves, in some cases). Perhaps it was enough to live them intensely. It is always afterwards that understanding comes.

On the other hand, it was most certainly appreciated by these prophets. From the time and background of Deuteronomy (after 750 B.C.), they made religious reading out of these separate traditions by gathering from sources both oral and written but separate what became a great prophetic history from Moses to the end of the kings.

Headlong conquest: Joshua

The first part of the book of Joshua (1-12) carries us along at breakneck speed in the wake of Joshua. He has hardly crossed Jordan dryfoot when the attack on Jericho begins; the town falls of itself; a road is opened up through mountainous country and Ai is taken;[1] Bethel surrenders and the Gibeonites send an embassy. A battle in the south, the five kings are put to death.[2] The conquests in the south are being recapitulated when the news breaks of victory in the north: Palestine is Israelite in its entirety. There is no time to narrate the battles, there is merely the list of enemy kings dead on the field of honor, two to the east of Jordan and thirty-one to the west.

The Holy Land is conquered and ready for surveying. The second part (Josh. 13-21) is good copy for a geography book suitable for young Israelites under King Josiah (640-609 B.C.).

The book concludes with three chapters of which number 24 is the important one (see Bible notes). The pact of Shechem at the end of the conquest is no doubt intended to bring into the covenant with God the Hebrews who did not go down into the land of Egypt in the old days with the patriarchs, and who by remaining in Palestine had no knowledge of the covenant on Sinai.

Prophetic history: the narrative is evidently schematic. The author is not carried away by his style. All Palestine conquered at one time? Well. Read on, the beginning of the next book (Judges); there the Hebrews, after opening the road upcountry by the odd victory, trickle rather thinly in between the cities of the Canaanites, making pacts, assimilating and hiring out to the enemy.

History very thin in facts. History marvelous in ground theme: the people of God following Jesus (or Joshua, the same root in Hebrew) meaning Yahweh-saves, and entering into possession of the land that was promised to their forefathers.

Is our life very humble too? Do we have the firm impression that the Church is standing still, even falling back on all fronts, geographical and sociological? What difference does that make? What is vital is to fight and keep faith; we are marching behind Jesus, invisibly but invincibly building the Promised Land, the world where God will be all in all.

When Agamemnon was fighting before Troy
(book of Judges)

This is one of those heart-stirring times when a new world is emerging from the upheaval. The period is that of Judges, from 1200 to 1050 B.C. approximately.

Since the great Semite invasion of the second millennium, the Middle East has found a new equilibrium, in about the thirteenth century. Three great powers split the world between them: the Assyria of the implacable soldiery to the east; the Egypt of the Seti and Rameses to the southwest; and the Hittites, to the north. The great Rameses II after his victory (his phrase) over them ca. 1280 B.C. finds himself obliged to sign the eternal pact with the Hittites, dividing the world. Equilibrium, peace; each can devote his energies to works that will immortalize his name.

1200 B.C.: **The peoples of the sea.** Entry of the Europeans into the Orient, coming from central Europe (?) like a tidal wave that is multiform. One group, the Dorians, puts an end to the dominion of the Acheans, takes Troy (? 1183) and settles in Greece. The rest come to grief on the shores of Egypt. Repulsed from there, they fan out along the whole Mediterranean coastline: Philistines in the land to which they will give their name, Palestine; Shardanes in Sardinia; Tursenoi in Italy where they become Etruscans, and many more.[3]

Against this background situation which is fluid, the book of Judges highlights some successful blows delivered by one or other of the twelve groups of Israelites, infiltrating between the fortified cities of the Canaanites and strongly challenged by some hulking fellows (and heavy beer-drinkers) in the persons of the Philistines. After the conquest under Joshua, each of the tribes took certain territory as best it might. Between them, no unity other than the common bond of religion. Perhaps a judge (called "petty" judge) chosen by each in turn, for purposes of settling their disputes. At all events, in times of stress a savior is raised up by God to save the situation. These action-stories, bragging on occasion, become the inheritance of the tribe. In at least one instance, one of them attains the level of great poetry, celebrating the victory of Deborah: it is the earliest Hebrew song that has come down to us (see Judg. 5; ca. 1124 B.C. according to Albright).

Popular history partisan and localized, it was a mine of information to the Deuteronomy author out to prove his theological contention some five or six centuries later; when you do good, God blesses you and when you do evil, God punishes you. In his expert hands, these scattered episodes organize themselves into a four-phase cycle, setting the pace of the whole work: (1) the people sin; so (2) God punishes them by sending an oppressor; (3) the people remember God and ask his aid; (4) God raises up a savior. The people are delivered. Then (1) they sin again; so (2), etc.

The pattern is monotonous and melancholy reading. But the religious meaning is rich textured. "Faith is not inherited. Each generation in turn faces a personal decision between the service of Baal (the false gods) and that of the living God. It is not only the history of Israel that is told in the process but also the history of the Church; it is our history. We enter forthwith into the great mystery of the patience of God" (S. de Dietrich).

"Incarnation of ideas by political fact" (books of Samuel and Kings).

Guy Belloncle was writing of Marxism. Perhaps it is even truer when transposed to Christianity. God has one idea for the world, to make it his Son's kingdom where we shall at length be men in the fullest sense, namely, the children of God. This idea for us Christians has turned all too often to the ideal of the individual. "One must work at being holy." Yet a thousand years of biblical history ought to have taught us the lesson that God puts people first and individuals second. God's idea: not to go fishing for saints but by means of them to build a kingdom of saints.

A false start: birth of royalty (Samuel cycle)

The Philistine threat made Israel turn to royalty, incidentally following the normal trend of historical evolution. God effected it through Samuel.

His mother, Hannah, was a holy woman; many turns of phrase in the song expressing her sentiments will appear again in the Magnificat of the Mother of God. Samuel's characteristic trait, his availability to God even before he actually knew him (that is, before he knew that God transcendent could also be very close to man and address himself to the heart), even when instinctively man is not in full agreement with what God asks him to perform.

Samuel remains the type of the prophet by whom God can act freely when he wants to make history. His true role, that of having assured the true religion on a lasting basis over a critical period; and by the choice of Saul as king and Saul's eventual replacement by David, having assured the foundation of a line of kings "after God's heart."

The history of Saul, the first king, emphasizes the dilemma of a leader torn between his loyalty to God (whose requirements are made known by men, whether it be prophets or church) and his need to rule effectively. His search for a compromise solution may be read about in 1 Sam. 13-15.

It marks the shift of emphasis, from Saul to David.

A dynamic kingdom, a king "drunk in the Lord": David

David is likeable. The most striking thing about him, his love of living. Whatever he does, he does wholeheartedly, whether sinning or loving, fighting or praying. Of choleric type, modern characterologists would say.

1 Sam. 16-31 describes his rise to power. Chosen by God because he was the smallest, a lad with red hair and marvelous eyes. "Do as I do, look into the heart" God told the aged Samuel, reticent. Spirited (for how he put his elder brother in his place, see 1 Sam. 17:26), danger-loving (Saul missed him for the "second time," 1 Sam. 18:11), full of faith (read about the fight with Goliath, 1 Sam. 17), a dynamic and chivalrous war-leader (1 Sam. 30:23), winner of men's allegiance and loved by all, his men want to follow him into battle (1 Sam. 26:7) and also into exile (2 Sam. 15:19). His friendship with Jonathan is legendary and to this day the children of Israel learn by heart the Song of the Bow (David's lament over Jonathan, 2 Sam. 1).

The second book of Samuel deals with David's accession to the throne. Capturing the city of the Jebusites, Jerusalem, he made it the capital of a united kingdom, taking to himself the two crowns: the north (Israel) and the south (Judah). He had to reconquer territory from the Philistines, then defend it against external enemies from Damascus to Amman and beyond.

His fondness for his own spoiled children brings about terrible family crises, clouding the closing years of his reign. Read if you will the magnificent story of the Davidic succession (2 Sam. 9; 1 Kings), written no doubt while the events were still news. Did the thought cross his mind as he climbed the Mount of Olives, persecuted by his kin, that one day a "son" of his line, Jesus, would do the very same thing, rejected by his own people?

"The king drunk in the Lord"

A very great deal could be said about the religion of David. See, for instance, 2 Sam. 6; 2 Sam. 24:24: "I will not offer my God a sacrifice that has cost me nothing." Special mention may be made of two aspects:

(a) **The sinful king** (2 Sam. 11-12). The man whose son Christ will one day proclaim himself, "son of David," is sinful, as we are, deeply so. Bible tradition will make of him the most saintly of the kings, at the same time not demuring from laying bare his wretchedness and his love of God in his wretchedness. Long before Christ would come and tell us that he lives in each brother of ours (Matt. 25), David sensed it. David sinned against a brother in having him killed so that he could have the man's wife. Suddenly realizing what he has done, he cries with the words of Ps. 51 that he has "sinned against none other than you, O God" (this conveys David's feelings and our own too).

(b) **The messianic king.** By his prophet Nathan (2 Sam. 7), God is going to make David aware (and make it fully clear to us, who know the Christ) that the final end of history is the building of the mystic body of Christ. David said to himself, "I live in a palace, a permanent structure, and my God has no temple. I will build him a house."

God says, No (remember the No's that God said to Abraham to make him surpass himself; the No's he says to us also). No! Your love is welcome but if you do build the temple you will risk thinking that everything has been accomplished and all is done, that God has a permanent home, the parish prospering and your branch of Catholic Action booming. You have done what you could; what remains is for you to learn that God alone sees to everything, far more than you can possibly conceive.

It is not you who is going to build a house (material, in space) but me, who will make a house (of the flesh, spiritual) for you in history. For God does not materially inhabit one place, he spiritually inhabits a faithful people (Congar).

The danger of settling down was not imagined.

Solomon: a king installed, a "Christian" at the top

The reign of David was all action. That of his son, a static one. It is made apparent too, in the account of his life. The first part, the "history of Solomon the great" (1 Kings 3-10) gives us a threefold view, presenting the threefold activity of an oriental king in ancient times:

1. Solomon the sage (1 Kings 3-5): the drama lies in his being "canonized" from the time of his accession (it is always dangerous to believe oneself arrived at sainthood too soon, as the second part will show).

2. Solomon the builder (1 Kings 6-8): palace, temple, garrison towns (the royal stables at Megiddo astonish the visitor to this day).

3. Solomon the trader (1 Kings 9-10): recently, his "factories" have been located near Aqaba and his copper mines.

The second part of the narrative presents a very different picture, the darker side of the reign: his many foreign wives brought the son of David to idolatry. In punishment: foreign foes cut into his land north and south while foes at home (Jeroboam in charge of all forced labor, and encouraged by a prophet) sharpen the division that on his death will split the kingdom into two, namely Judah and Israel. The united kingdom lasted only eighty years.

But when time has distilled history, the unpleasant side will be forgotten and Solomon will remain the type of the wise man. Wise because so he was, and the Bible attributes to him 3,000 proverbs and 1,005 psalms. An exaggeration; but there is no reason to deny him some of the sayings in the book of Proverbs. Later, to give a book his label meant to say that it followed the literary genre of Wisdom (see, for example, Eccles., Wisd., Sir., etc.). Wise too because he made his court a literary center. After the fashion of his father-in-law (well, one of them!), the pharaoh, Solomon surrounded himself with prophets and sages, scribes and annalists. It is from his reign that the beginning of Hebrew literature may be dated.

Beginning of history and theology

The reader may recall how, from the time of Abraham, the old tribal tales, constantly added to, found willing hearers. Since then, the life of Moses was a new fount of material for this treasure trove of extracts from the law, poetry, and narratives. More recently, the life of David contributed further episodes. It was tempting for a scribe (a single scribe or a school of them?) to rearrange the corpus and try to make a history. This explains the probable origin of what is known as the Yahwist document (or tradition).

If you marked the different traditions with different colored pencils in the margins of your Bible, look again at the Yahwist history and discover its charm, which is unique.[4] You will find there a profoundly human God living divine history with his people.

It all starts with **Abraham**. God chose for himself a friend who loves him in return, totally trusting. Because he loves God, God tests him to make his love progress. The Yahwist finds himself moved in telling this plain tale of God's love among men. But what now, men tire of being loved: sin! Communion with God is broken: the people live in bondage in Egypt. So God starts again, taking his people out of servitude to bring them back to his service. By **Moses** love is found again, but love no longer with the spontaneity of Abraham, love threatened without respite by the temptation of truckling to the false gods of Canaan.[5]

That is the story, as fine as a poem, told us by the Yahwist. Historian he may be, he is also a theologian: he wants to understand. Abraham. It marks the beginning of the history of his people. But the beginning of history? Of history pure and simple.

Then the sacred author inspired by God, perhaps drawing on the traditions (of his people or others) wrote what may be the finest chapters of the Bible: history of the origins.[6]

History of the origins

What did our Yahwist know about it? Nothing except that God, eternally the same, ought not to have acted differently with mankind from what he did with that part of mankind forming his people. Perhaps it is in thinking of the history of his people that the author, guided by the Holy Spirit, wrote this wondrous history of mankind. Everything began by God's love to man—Abraham; thus by God's love to the man—Adam. For him, too, God chose a land, the earthly paradise. To increase his stature in love, he too was tested, and man, like the people later, loved not. He preferred the love of false gods to God's love. What more eloquent image could a ninth-century writer produce than that of man turning away from God to follow the advice of the serpent, the serpent that the Canaanites were in fact adoring to the Yahwist's own knowledge and that his people were being constantly tempted to adore? Man had become the slave of the land he should have ruled. But since God is forgiveness, he let man have his love once more. Adam after the Fall loves still. No longer with the spontaneity of Abraham's love, the spontaneity of the earthly paradise, however, but the love of obedience from an upright people, the faith of the man who, as St. Paul was to express it, finds God guided by the hard taskmaster of commandment and law (Rom. 7).

Everything has been said with these definitive pages. From the episodic history of the people, the Yahwist, because he is a "prophet," was able to extract—and project backwards to the origins in the language of imagery— the essential concerning God's behavior toward men, and mankind's response.

Further, ages without end were to find teaching therein. Paul one day was going to find clearly written the mystery of original sin (Rom. 5) and John the vision of the lasting Kingdom, of the eternal garden where we shall taste the fruit of the tree of life (Rev. 2:7); the Church was to discover the whole history of our redemption stemming from the "proto-evangelium" (Gen. 3:15), while each of us sees the story of his infancy passionately loved by the Father but in whose infant heart Satan so often arrives, introducing doubt and destroying confidence: "God said? . . . not at all: you will be as gods!" Eternal temptation to make ourselves gods when it is enough to accept simply and let ourselves be loved by him to become a child of God.

2 **Yahweh Thundering, His Love Rejected** (Amos, Hosea Isaiah, Micah)

Ivory palace reception: Jeroboam II gives a press conference (the prophet Amos reports)

The date is 750 B.C., the place Samaria in the summer palace. King Jeroboam II highlights the situation; that is to say, he listens to the annalists of the kingdom singing his praises. A lot has changed since the time of Jeroboam I; on the death of Solomon in 935 B.C., he raised against the legitimate heir of David (who kept the two tribes of the south and the capital Jerusalem) ten of the twelve tribes of Israel, creating the kingdom of the north (or Israel). There had been three great powers in the Middle East; of these, Egypt is in full decadence, the Hittites a forgotten name; only Assyria still gives a moment's cause for alarm: also decadent for some while, from 900 this power attempted to reimpose authority. Happily one of Jeroboam's predecessors, King Ahaz, turned the tables. In 854 B.C. at Qarqar he halted the advance of the great Salmanazar III with his 2,000 chariots and 10,000 soldiers (and the help, it is true, of some other kings). Palace intrigues since then weakened Assyria. Another contender, the kingdom of Damascus by ambition and also topographically forms a firstrate buffer. So joy and gladness are the order of the day. Peace has been made with their southern brothers; under the lead of the wise Uzziah, they too bask in momentary splendor.

Material prosperity had never reached such a pitch. The walls covered with finely carved ivory rang to the sound of the harp. Through windows of alabaster, past the green groves of olive and over the hillsides clad in fig trees, could be seen the Mediterranean. The sky was very blue. The great ladies propped themselves languidly on couches covered in ebony, calling to their husbands, "Bring us something to drink!" The notables paid no heed, sprawling on their divans, anointed with the finest oils, "they dine on lambs from the flock"; "they drink wine by the bowlful."

Of course, this prosperity was not without penalties. But the wall separating the upper class from the hovels of the people was a solid one. The cry of the poor man as he was crushed or the little one sold for a pair of sandals, these could never be heard through such a wall.

So God thundered: "Yahweh roars," etc.

Lifting the heavy drapes aside, a man enters: a country-man, his feet still dirty from the pastures where Yahweh came upon him. The great ladies listen, aghast: "Listen, you cows, lolling in Samaria: Jeroboam will die by the sword and Israel suffer sentence of exile."

The Gravediggers of the Kingdom

> "From remote times, the prophets who preceded you and me prophesied war, famine and plague—but the prophet who prophesies peace can only be recognized as one truly sent by Yahweh when his word comes true."
>
> Jeremiah in 593 B.C.

Enough to say that though hope may always be included, the message of the prophets in the eighth and seventh centuries B.C. is a gloomy one. Only after the disaster of exile does it become comforting. In other words, when everything is going fine, the prophet cries, "Woe!" and when woe comes, he talks of peace. This paradoxical attitude of God is not unmotivated. The covenant with his people contained unbreakable promises of well-being on God's part and faithfulness exacted on the part of the people. Now when everything is humming, they will have nothing but the promises: since God gave his word and can accomplish anything, he ought to look after his people. God is going to make them realize the hard way that the covenant must first be kept by them.

"The prophets of the eighth and seventh centuries had the task of waking the people-elect from their false sense of security. **Israel settled in the Promised land, settled in possessions, settled in victories, settled in institutions and settled in faith. From the moment they thought the goal was reached, they began to lose their souls.** They were subtly won over by the Canaan environment and compromised with their gods, customs, and institutions. They sought military security in strength of chariots, political security in foreign alliances, spiritual security in sacrifices offered to Baal with one hand and to the Eternal Father with the other.

"A strange certainty took hold of the prophets: **for Israel to find God again, they must lose everything else;** everything else meant their material security, everything which willy-nilly had taken the place of the living God in their hearts; it meant riches and glory as a free and independent people; it meant the soil, the line of kings, even the Holy City deemed inviolable and the temple too, visible sign of the presence of God. Israel had to go back to the Wilderness, to the trials of solitude where having nothing of their own, they might learn to hold on to God alone" (S. de Dietrich, **God's Plan**).

Amos
The Covenant: A Responsibility Shared

> "You alone of all the families of earth have I acknowledged, therefore it is for all your sins I mean to punish you."
>
> Amos 3:2

God does not love the dry-as-dust intellectual. When he speaks through man, he starts by entering his life and putting him through his paces before letting him proclaim the pith of what he has learned.

The beginning of Amos is impressive (1:2). He does not express a revelation but a "perception of meeting God. It is the cry of a man who has met God" (A. Neher).

Amos has left us two other witnesses to his vocation: 7:14-15 is circumstantial and 3:3-8 tries to give us some insight into the heart of prophecy (an irresistible meeting with God, and a step forward with him, introducing man to his plan).

Arriving in the flourishing kingdom of Israel, this rough diamond from the wilderness of Judah understands as he delivers the message what God has made him realize. The people of God, the people of the covenant with God, have used the covenant as an automatic assurance of well-being. Amos must make them recall that the covenant is, first and foremost, a shared responsibility. In the covenant made on Sinai, God gave an undertaking insofar as Israel did likewise: sharing responsibility, "where each receives his part from the joint operation," but which is not real unless each "does his part" (A. Neher).

The whole of Amos' job: to make Israel recall its share of responsibility.

This part, says Amos, is simple: they must use justice toward God. No cult ("the calves you offer me, your sacrifices and your songs . . . I like them not"), but justice. What is this justice toward God? Listen carefully: it is the first time God speaks so clearly, and his Son will be mindful of it when he decrees the Last Judgment

(Matt. 25:31-46). Justice toward God means practicing justice among men.

This is the inner meaning of the message of Amos: the vertical relationship of man-to-God passes through the dimension which is horizontal of man-to-man. One day we shall know the reason why: in each of our brethren, loved or rejected, the Son of man is mysteriously present. Amos, of course, was unaware of it. But never before (David perhaps?) had it been so clearly sensed and said that to be true to the covenant with God meant turning not to him but to brother men, that this part of the responsibility held in common with God and to which we have been bidden meant in the end the building of a brotherhood kingdom.

If it is not possible for us to forget it, then doubtless the debt is owed initially to Amos, the prophet of justice.

Notes for further reading:
The literary forms most frequently found in the prophets are exhortation and oracle. Amos 1-2 gives a very good example of the second type, attaining perfection from the start.

Amos 3:12. With his own vivid touch Amos embarks on the theme of the Remnant, see a note to Isa. 4:3, which will help you follow it through the Bible.

Amos 3:15. Visit the Louvre, when you are in Paris. In the department of oriental antiquities, some ivories are displayed from the palace of Hazael, King of Damascus, nearly contemporary with Amos. (To get the most out of the visit, first read the little book of A. Parrot, published by Delachaux & Niestlé, entitled **The Louvre and the Bible**.)

Amos 4. Punishments, proof that the love of God pursues man; when immured in quietude, only suffering can draw him out and make him face the big decisions.

Amos 4:13; 5:8-9; 9:5-6. Doxologies on a par with the finest hymns to nature.

Amos 5:4-6. The search for God, one of the most profound spiritual attitudes of the Bible, expressing the longing of every religious soul for the beloved Lord.

Amos 7-9. The prophet in his role of special pleading (remembering Moses).

Amos 9:11-15. God's final aim, to re-erect the house of David, the mystic body of the Son (cf. Acts 15:16-17).

HOSEA
The Unadulterated Love of God

For us men to understand, we need to see. This raised a problem for God: how to make us understand he loves us? So God had a look round creation for what was the most beautiful of all he had made.[8] He found two things: the tenderness, fresh as the dew, of an engaged couple made him pause and consider, That is how I love my people; the other thing was a mother enfolding her child, and God understood that for us he too had the "tenderness of a mother."

At the time when Amos of Judah was preaching in the northern kingdom, a man called Hosea was living there. He may have been an ordinary landowner; he was a man of passionate soul, tender and rough both together.

God said to him, "Go, find a girl and love her. Have children. Your tenderness for her and your love for them will be a sign for my people: it is thus and more that I love them, . . ." Or rather, that is what God would have liked to tell Hosea. But unfortunately he knew that his people—that we men—love him not, and that instead of responding to his impassioned love we would rather play around with false gods whether Baal of the Canaanites or ourselves. . . . Hosea loving a young girl, when the image was not a suitable one. . . . God found another image, far more tragic and revelatory of his love.

God said to Hosea, "Go, marry a whore, and get children with a whore, for the country itself has become nothing but a whore by abandoning Yahweh."

A son, God names him "Unloved," and another, "No-people-of-mine."

Hosea loving a whore; God loving his people. God ponders this and in the extraordinary second chapter, considering what has been done with his love, the words that blaze from his lips are those of a wronged husband. Then he calls to mind the beginning of his covenant with Israel when the people, in the Wilderness and in want, relied wholly on God and loved him: the time of the engagement. A marvelous certainty impresses itself upon him: his bride-to-be will come back to him because he has loved her so completely. His love is so strong that he will give a virgin heart back to the sinning woman.

Now the heart of God is known and when his Son comes down to earth, from the outset he will be recognized. The father of the prodigal son, Luke clearly states, is the God of Hosea (cf. Hos. 2 and Luke 15); there is no better illustration of the message of Hosea than the tale of the sinful woman loved by Jesus and forgiven because she was loved (Luke 7:36-50).[9]

The heart of God is known and human love is the sacrament thereof. From Hosea onward, a boy and girl loving were bound to call to mind the tenderness with which God loves us.[10] "This mystery," St. Paul will say of marriage, "has many implications; but I am saying it applies to Christ and the church" (Eph. 5:32).

Guide to further reading:

Three ideas, the threads of which run through the text:

1. The love of God the Father is strong, like that of a husband.

"Existential" face of love: God's love points the way to Israel.

Hos. 9:11-17. God is the one who gives life. Without him, mankind is ruined, wrongdoers and without fruit (9:16, a play on words for Ephraim and fruit come from the same root).

Hos. 14:5-9. "It is my doing that you bear fruit."

Affective faces of love: God's fatherly love, 9:1-9; 7:15 (cf. Deut. 1:31).

God's motherly love; in Hebrew, the word for God's love toward us is the same as for the mother's breast. See Luke 1:78, from the Benedictus, "by the tender mercy of our God." (Have another look at the note on p. 31.) This tender mercy may now be found on every page.

(When I pray, do I realize I am praying to one who is "deeply moved" thinking of me? Jer. 31:20).

God's nuptial love, the educative face of love. Not paternal love, which gives regardless. God gives himself to man made in his image so that by free acceptance and enrichment, man may find fulfillment, as husband and wife in each other.

(Do I think of God and the Lord Jesus with the same tenderness of a promised bride for the one she loves?)

2. The response of Israel, an adulterous love.

The response God expects is tenderness or, rather, the untranslatable term, **hesed** (see note to Hos. 2:21). God knows because his love is overpowering that one day his people will return it, Hos. 2:21-22 (see Eph. 5:27). For the time being, Israel knows the love, but—

The love is adulterous for the false gods and makes them as "hateful as the thing they loved" (9:10).

3. The love of God is creative, pure love.

God loves us not because we are good but so that we shall become good. His love is not only a giving (like the delirious joy, untried, of the engagement) but a for-giving (giving-plus, in the clear redeeming love after failing).

If sin is essentially a breaking with God, redemption is primarily a returning to God. Be very careful of the word "returning"; it is one of the biblical ways ("the" way for St. John) of talking about salvation. The returning has three phases:

(a) In the first place, awareness of state of sin.

God who made us, unhelped by us, cannot save us without help from us. The feeling must have life within us, however imperfectly, that we are wretched away from God (Hos. 2:9; 6:1-3; 7:14. See also Luke 15:17 and Exod. 2:23).

Salutary punishment has no other purpose but to make us feel that sin does not pay. God leaves us as naked as the day we were born (2:9-11; 3:5; 4:10; 5:14-15; 8:7).

(b) The returning.

If we can stand our wretchedness then there is no way back to God because our sins hem us in, 5:4; 7:2 (the nearest approximation to hell and the infernal face of sin). God must himself seek us out, like a shepherd his sheep (2:6). There is no returning to God except on the shoulders of Christ crucified.

(c) Love found again. The new covenant.

The changing of the names of Hosea's children is the guarantee (2:25). It means total recovery, "I will heal their disloyalty" (14:5); the engagement will last forever.

—   —   —   —   —

We now leave the northern kingdom for Jerusalem, to

hear what the prophet Isaiah says. But first, something must be said about a book which saw the light of day about a century after Isaiah's time.

DEUTERONOMY

"I would not have loved the Lord had he not first
  loved me,
Who can be understanding love except the one
  who is loving,
I love the beloved and my heart is loving him"
                    3rd ode of Solomon, ca. A.D. 100

Deuteronomy: the finest poem to the love of God.

It is presented in the form of three discourses of Moses, exhorting the people prior to arrival in the Holy Land. It in fact deals with the law of Moses in a re-edited version ("Deuteronomy" meaning "law the second time around"). This was owing to new historical circumstances and the development of religious thinking. The original law was given to a people with tribal structures, living in subtribes in the wilderness. Now the time had come for the people to become town-dwellers. It also comes about that, in revising the law, the people are no longer able to speak of it in quite the same terms as before. For in the meanwhile, through Hosea, they have learned that the contract binding them to God, the covenant, is one of love, a marriage bond.

The work was done in the northern kingdom, in the Levite environment (they were "dedicated to the service of God"), nurtured on the thinking of Hosea (and later Jeremiah); the code of law was conveyed by them at the time of the fall of the northern kingdom to Jerusalem in 721 B.C. Embedded among the temple archives, it was "discovered" there in 622 during the reign of the holy king Josiah (2 Kings 22-23). The primitive code with later additions has become what is now known as Deuteronomy,[11] according to a general consensus of opinion.

Deuteronomy spoke of God's love for his people as nothing previously had. The "Shema Israel" (see Deut. 6:4ff.) remains the morning prayer of the devout Jew, and a goodly number have gone to their deaths with these words upon their lips, murmured or spoken loud. Remember the final page of "The Last of the Just."

For a first reading, you may bear in mind two words, echoing throughout like a theme: the key words "love" and "remember."

1. "Listen, Israel . . . you shall love the Lord your God with all your heart . . ." etc.

God loves us. With no strings attached. He has chosen, elected Israel from among all nations, for no merit on their part, indeed in spite of (one might almost say, because of) their sins (Deut. 4:32-40; 7:7-8; 9; 14:1-2; 32:6-11).

He loves us with a demanding love, "jealous." If he tests his people, it is to see if they can withstand tempting, to see if his training is successful, if the child can walk unaided: Deut. 1:29-33; 2:7; 8:1-6 (God knows the father's concern when he tries out his son and wonders, Will he make it? O father, we are little children, not very sure of our love, so **ne nos inducas in tentationem,** "lead us not into temptation"); if he punishes the people, it is to bring them back to him after sin by suffering: Deut. 4:29-31.

God's love encourages us to respond to his love, by loving him with a respectful love (this is what the word for "fear" means in the Bible: "respectful love," "adoration full of affection"; watch out for meanings when the word "fear" occurs referring to God, e.g., Deut. 10:12-13;

11:13-22); it also encourages us to respond by loving others. Marvelous delicacy of Deut. 15. The response itself is a grace from God, Deut. 30.

The response for us is life (11:26-32; 30:15-20). Existential face of this response (the most dramatic theme of St. John's Gospel).

2.   Remember . . .

Importance of remembering, it transforms my whole life to a gift, a sacrifice to God. **Unde et memores,** etc. "This is why we remember . . . ," said during consecration, in the Anamnesis.

Deuteronomy is a paradox. It presents itself like a promise from God: "When you get to the holy land, I will give you the fruits," etc. It has an air (but only an air) of forgetting it was composed a good while after entry into possession of these fruits! What God promises me is nothing other than this basket of fruit in my hands. These fruits are the object of God's promise, a gift. But because I possess them and have plucked them myself, I run a strong risk of forgetting they are a gift, seeing only the fruit of my efforts there instead. For them to become again what in reality they are (a "giving"), I must remember, must recall the history of them. In Deut. 26, for instance, the whole sacrifice and ceremony of the offering consists solely in remembering. The bread the priest has in his hands, that is one thing. From the moment he remembers all about it, it becomes a gift transformed by the power of memory, the Anamnesis.

It was easy for the people to receive the manna as a gift from God. It came harder to them to receive in the same way, as a gift, the fruits of the earth. And yet they were only what was yielded after the manna (Josh. 5:12).

May the reading of Deuteronomy so touch our hearts with love of God that we may be taught to make our lives, the fruits of our activities and those of mankind (science and progress) what they are in reality, a gift from God; and teach us also to receive ourselves humbly as a gift, the most marvelous, of God's love.

ISAIAH

A Baedeker of Jerusalem . . .

Jerusalem has not been mentioned since Solomon. A lot has changed. We need a guide, and here is Isaiah. Let us go with him and he will show us around the town, which he knows very well. Here are the ramparts and the towers at the corners; the temple where God lives and the priests who do his business at the altar; down below, the waters of Siloah babbling softly, the little streets where walk the "daughters of Sion with their heads held high and enticing eyes, the way they mince along, tinkling the bangles on their feet." A plume of smoke from the neighboring valley (Isaiah's eyes blaze wrath), the new-born are being sacrificed again to a Canaanite god. There is an Assyrian altar (in the Holy City) at the street corner, and then we are at the palace. Isaiah has free access. Everyone says Hello to him; sometimes the king listens to what he has to say on the subject of foreign policy, for no one is a sounder judge of peoples and good allies.

The year is 740 B.C. Uzziah, the good leper king, has not long died. His son, who had been regent, takes his place on the throne. The country is doing fine. But for five years now Tiglath-Pileser III has been ruler of Assyria.

Isaiah's age is twenty, maybe twenty-five. His birth and noble nature mark him out for a bright political future.

God is going to make a prophet of him.

"No one can see God and survive"

God is the living God—to the point that contact with him spells death, like contact with a high-voltage cable. Our frame cannot cope with such terrible energy. The living God is too much for us. He is "All-other" beside us (the Bible calls him "holy," meaning "apart"). "It is a dreadful thing to fall into the hands of the living God" will be written in the letter to the Hebrews (10:31). "We are certain to die, because we have seen God"; such is the instinctive cry of the faithful in the presence of God transcendent (Judg. 13:15-22), and God himself decided to put holy terror into the hearts of his people, meaning respect, the first step in loving (turn back to 2 Sam. 6 and 1 Sam. 6:20).

("Let us put ourselves in the presence of God"— prayers used to begin like that. Am I aware of what I think I am doing "in the presence of God"? The living God is nothing like the Good Lord or Child Jesus, and Christ cannot be chums with us unless he is first the terrible God for us. This does not prevent intimacy but, rather, leads to it. Love has two components: respect and intimacy. Is he sure, the chap who wants to get on terms of intimacy with his promised bride without respecting her, that he is not simply after "possessing" the girl?)

"No one can see God and survive." And if we now as Christians have access to God, it is because mankind is in effect dead from contact with God: in the terrible death on the Cross, mankind is dead in the person of him who is at once both man and God. But in him, too, mankind is given life again. And each of us, in him, by baptism.

"No one can see God and survive." Few men have been reserved the privilege of seeing him and surviving.

They were all marked, as a result. The Bible names Moses (Exod. 3; 33-34), Elijah (1 Kings 19) and Isaiah.[12]

Isaiah "sees" God (Isa. 6)

Isaiah is in the temple when suddenly the familiar scene fades. Sensed behind the veil concealing the Holy of Holies, the cherubim protecting the Ark with their golden wings come to life and Isaiah "sees" God.[13] He immediately perceives the holiness of God and his transcendence (holy, "apart," threefold and to infinity); while the experience lasts, he has the feeling that he cannot stand before God:

● contact with "All-other," the living one who fills our poor lives to bursting with glory;

● contact with "All-pure," at once revealing and destroying the sinning which is affliction of the flesh.

In a flash, Isaiah understands his only chance of salvation, to lean on God or better, let God stand by him (Isa. 7:9). "If you do not rely on me, then I shall not stand by you"; this is Isaiah's catchphrase (see 10:20).

Isaiah sent by God

By this contact with God, Isaiah realized in a twinkling that he was both lost (because mortal and a sinner) and saved (because his faith turned him to God who sustained him).

But what of the people? His people also standing in the presence of the living God, and sinning. In danger of death permanently, and heedless. Who is going to wake them up and bring them back from death to life, by this burning touch. "Whom shall I send?" is what God says. "Here I am, send me."

Isaiah receives this terrible mission from God (a bit like all prophets): to make his brothers realize they are living in God's presence; the choice before them, inevitably:

● either to rely on themselves, "the" sin for Isaiah, pride, and this means punishment and death;

● or else to rely on God in humility of faith, and God lets Isaiah know that very few of his fellowmen are going to make the right choice. The "remnant" who will be rescued from disaster and "sanctified" by God may be pitifully few, but they will be the bearers of great hopefulness.

So God is going to stand in the path of his people:

● as a stumbling stone (Isa. 8:14) against which they will be brought down and perish;

● or as a foundation stone (Isa. 28:16) that with the help of faith, the true people of God may come into being.

This is the twofold mission Isaiah receives, a hard face to the people and grace for the small Remnant (Isa. 6:9-13).

(a) God the stumbling stone

Through Isaiah, the people become aware that he lives in contact with God the Holy One. The majority harden, refusing God and pretending to be able to get along by relying on themselves and their own resources, with help if need be from their allies Egypt or Assyria. "The" sin, the everlasting sin of pride (Isa. 2:6-22; 8:5-8; 9:8-12; 10:12; 22:9-11; 31:1).

So the People as people will be destroyed (Isa. 5:24; 10:17).

God's disappointment may be measured from reading

the magnificent verses concerning his love for the "vine" (Isa. 5:1-7).

Jesus too will be a stumbling stone (Luke 2:34), but John will tell us that the "true" vine, the faithful one is Jesus and us in him (John 15).

(b) The Messiah the foundation stone

The Remnant of those who escape ruin comprise the faithful whose only trust is in God (Isa. 7:3; 10:20-21).

The Remnant become holy as God is holy (4:3; 6:13) and constitute the new people of God, the true Israel (which the Church continues) (Isa. 4:2-4; 28:5-6).

This new Israel, Isaiah sees already on the way with the birth of Emmanu-El (God-with-us). This baby means no doubt in the first place Hezekiah, son of the young king Ahaz but insofar as may be, in advance, a figure of the Messiah. Isaiah was probably not aware of this, but the Holy Spirit is also the text's author (refer back to plenary meaning, p. 24.

This Book of Emmanu-El, as it has been called, is justifiably the most celebrated of all the book of Isaiah. It contains three texts in particular:

● announcing the birth of Emmanu-El (Isa. 7:10-14). "Now God is no longer with you, Ahaz, or with you, house of David [meaning the people as a nation] but with us, his faithful people." (Read Luke 1:26; Matt. 1:23.)

● with his birth, like a light in darkness, a marvelous kingdom is coming to fulfill what has been promised (Isa. 8:21-9:9). (Read Luke 1:78; 2:9-10, 29-34; John 8—"I am the light of the world," etc.)

● this royal birth will be the beginning of messianic

times (effectively starting with Jesus), marvelous as paradise regained (Isa. 11:1-9). (Read Luke 2:14; 4:17.)

MICAH
(Mi-ka-yah, Who-like-God?)

Micah is from Moresheth. Have a look at the map of Palestine and you will see what that means. The senseless policy of the ruling powers (sheltered for the time being behind the walls of their capitals) had brought the Assyrian army on the warpath into the area four times in the course of a few years, namely, in 734, 720, 711, and 701 B.C. The Assyrian army meant death and destruction, ruin and rape, plunder and deportations. Micah came from Moresheth, a village. So the exactions of the great powers were being made on his people. His name from birth indicated he would one day go and tell Jerusalem, with God to guide, and this he did. No doubt the aristocrat Isaiah was preaching there. Micah's message was equally tragic, although told in another tone. He lacked the consummate skill of Isaiah but had suffered in the flesh with his brethren from the injustices he came to condemn; he suffered in the spirit to see no longer did anyone believe in the true God alone. His cry to the city lacked fine phrasing and polish, but it spoke of suffering and what God thought.

And in the Church, world without end, each Good Friday the tale is taken up again of a suffering God whom none loved (Mic. 6:3-4).

Micah had nothing good to say about the rich; they had no understanding of the brotherly love that membership of the same covenant ought to kindle: landowners (2:1-10), rulers (3:1-4) and venal prophets (3:5-8), all the rich people who did their building with the blood of the poor (3:9-10)—(forgive me, but after that I can no longer admire with a perfectly good conscience the great works of ancient and modern art, the Parthenon and our monuments, etc.)—the trader who cheats (6:10-11) and the people who no longer know what love is (3:11; 7:3-6).

The people are so perverted that the day will come when they will want to return to God and will no longer even know that what God wants is love. Micah will then come out with his own definition (6:8) of the three basic requirements of the love of God as transmitted by Amos, Hosea, and Isaiah.

What is good has been explained to you man.

This is what Yahweh asks of you: only this, to **act justly** (the message of Amos entirely); to **love tenderly** (what Hosea emphasized); and to walk humbly with your God (as Isaiah did).

Micah would rank as a very great prophet even had we nothing else of his but this ability to synthesize and arrive at this unified vision of life. It is this vision which gives true meaning to all his reproaches; what he seeks is for a united People of God to come into being, loving all and beloved.

"Who is like God?" All others will grow weary and cause destruction in the end. But not God. The other side of ruin, Micah glimpses the Kingdom of God on the way; his one thought then is of the Messiah who is going to reign over Israel and of the person who will be his mother (Mic. 5).[14]

3 **"A Scream Like That of a Woman in Labour"** (Jeremiah, Zephaniah, Nahum, Habakkuk)

> Yes, I hear screams like those of a
>   woman in labour,
> anguish like that of a woman giving
>   birth to her first child;
> they are the screams of the daughter of
>   Sion gasping,
> hands outstretched,
> "Ah, I despair! I am fainting away
> with murderers surrounding me."
>
> Jer. 4:31

All Jeremiah is in these words. The suffering of his people (personified in the daughter of Zion, that is, Jerusalem), is his own. He knows that the people, as people, must die: he will tell them so, in plain terms; his message is from God.

It must be, in order that a new People, the People of the new covenant, may arise and adore God "in spirit and in truth."

> but when she has given birth to the child she forgets
>   the suffering
> in her joy that a man has been born into the world.
>
> John 16:21

Joy is everywhere in Jeremiah. For himself it will only be a certainty and a dream.

"Do not say, 'I am a child.' . . . Go now . . ."

The calling of Isaiah is extraordinary: a blazoning forth in the temple, God, the cherubim, and the spontaneity of the great personage ready to take on responsibilities.

Nothing of that appears in Jeremiah. It is all simple. "As of a man used to being in contact with God, in his inner life, without extraordinary visions. In their dialogue, God and his prophet seem to treat one another as equals and talk to each other as friend to friend."

Jeremiah, priest of a little village near Jerusalem, shy and sensitive, made for hearth and home, to love and be loved.

But in his mouth henceforth (his, Jeremiah's!) there will be no more words, only the Word created of God.

Word that will be heard by all nations and kingdoms.

Word that destroys sin and the man who clings to it: "to tear out and overthrow."

Word that creates: "to build and to sow seed."

Solitary, poor in human terms, with a sole certainty: "I am with you," Yahweh has said. Jeremiah, witness in the world of what God can do when a "poor man" gives his love wholly to him. "In my weakness is my strength," St. Paul will say, "in him who is my strength I can do all things."

In this, Jeremiah is the model and first instance of the type of spiritual poverty referred to by Zephaniah.

ZEPHANIAH

When his voice is heard, ca. 640-630 B.C. (it is sixty years since Isaiah's voice fell silent), it is to proclaim that the time has come: a day is dawning, when God will destroy his people. "A day of wrath": "dies irae, dies illa" (1:15). Wrath of God which is going to fall on all sinners, on Judah first, but eventually on all of them whether north or south, west or east.

Zephaniah gives the why and wherefore for this outburst of wrath: God's disappointment in love. He sought "in the midst" of Jerusalem or "in his bosom" (the same word in Hebrew, the key to Zephaniah) someone who trusted in him. Nobody! In the midst of Jerusalem, there is only one just being, only one, and that is God! He makes up his mind to purify the city by suffering.

The result will be twofold, and God will think nothing of "dancing with shouts of joy for you as on a day of festival" over his purified city (3:17).

(1) In the midst of it, there will be found only a humble and lowly people (3:12), those who know how to become poor in the sight of God as in the sight of Assyria or their creditors. Zephaniah returns to the terms of material poverty but transfigures them. They stand for a setback; he makes them a prayer. "He calls his contemporaries to this spiritual poverty, so-termed, meaning the faith with stress laid on abandonment, humility and absolute trust" (A. Gelin).[15] From then on, the ideal of the poor men, the **anawim** will never lose its appeal to the best in Israel. Their charter one day will be the Magnificat.

(2) In the midst of it, there God will be! In her bosom, that of the daughter of Zion, Jerusalem, God will find a home.

Zephaniah's enthusiasm for what will come to pass is only matched by the deep well of joy in the lady by whom it is to be accomplished. In the fullness of time, a daughter of Zion, poor and small, will carry her God in her bosom, and he will be made poor too. St. Luke bears this out, telling the story of the Incarnation in words of Zephaniah's. Compare Zeph. 3:14-18 and Luke 1:28-33:

God's announcement to the "daughter of Sion"	God's announcement by the angel to Mary
Shout for joy daughter of Zion . . .	Rejoice, so highly favored
the king of Israel, Yahweh,	[her new name]

is in your midst . . .
Zion, have no fear
Yahweh, your God
is in your midst
a victorious warrior.

The Lord is with you
[Yahweh trans. into
            Greek] . . .
Mary, do not be afraid
you are to conceive and bear
a son and you must name him
"Yahweh saves"
            [meaning Jesus]
he will rule . . . .

But this joy belongs to the time to come. The present reality means the day of wrath. God speaks and makes this accusation,

> for I am determined to gather the nation, . . .
> and to pour out my fury on you.
>
> Zeph. 3:8

The nations are already on the move.

100 years of terror in the Middle East

> ". . . for who has not felt your unrelenting cruelty . . ."
>
> Nah. 3:19

Reverberating through the book of Nahum like the stroke from a gong, this cry of hate is astonishing. To understand, better than attempting explanations, refer to the twin volumes of A. Parrot in the "Universe of Forms" series. The civilization of Sumer (Abraham left it) was a hard one but produced those admirable statues with great eyes open on the infinite and the mysterious smile, akin to archaic Greek work or the statue-columns of Chartres. Then Assyria succeeded it. Not a statue of a woman (well, just one!), only brute force, "horses fiercer than wolves in the dark," implacable warriors "slaughtering nations without pity," "sinful, he who makes his own strength his god" (Hab. 1).

A hundred years have gone by since Amos and Jeroboam. A hundred years of terror. Like a canker with many tentacles, the Assyrian empire stretched to the Mediterranean. In 721 B.C. Samaria fell and the inhabitants were deported. Sargon II got as far as Cyprus. In 701, Jerusalem and its king, hemmed in by Sennacherib like a "caged bird," were delivered only by Isaiah's entreaty for help from above, and this is borne out by the historian Herodotus. Assarhadon received tribute from the king of Tyre and that of Judah, the wicked Manasseh. In 669, the literate king Ashurbanipal (his library with the firstrate inventory is famous) came to the throne. It marked the high point of the empire and the beginning of the end also. He went from the scene ca. 630. After him, a row of degenerate rulers, some reverses through blows from Babylonians and Medes. Assyria fell, then Nineveh in 612, and the whole Middle East could breathe again and cry for joy, albeit the joy was mingled with hatred.

NAHUM

The little book of Nahum (ca. 612 B.C.) provides the finest example. With extraordinary evocative power (the chariots storming through the streets of Nineveh, gripping to read), he shows us how God takes charge of history. This is the theme of the psalm which opens, and sets the key for, the book, contrasting God's anger over wrongdoing and his faithfulness toward those who trust in him.

> There is no remedy for your wound, [king of Assyria]
> All who hear the news of you
> clap their hands at your downfall.
>
> Nah. 3:19

The Middle East delightedly applauding. But they were only changing one master for another. The general in

command of the Babylonian troops was Nebuchadnezzar.
In 605, the Battle of Carchemish marked the start of
Babylonian attacks on Palestine, with a few months respite
only when the new king was crowned in Babylon.

HABAKKUK

The prophet Habakkuk (from 605 to 597) is an amazed
witness. He understands that these Babylonians (the
"Chaldeans") have been God's instruments in overthrowing
Assyria. But they are no less cruel! How can God who is
pure use such impure means? "This is the problem of
evil at national level and Habakkuk is scandalized, just
like a lot of present-day people" (R. de Vaux). The new
element lies in the fact of Habakkuk daring—the first man
so to do—to call God to account for his management of
world affairs.

God's answer (the same will soon be given to Job too)
brings us face to face with "All-other"; it is to be basic
to the theology of St. Paul, "the upright man will live by
his faithfulness" (Hab. 2:4).

When one no longer understands, there is only one
thing to do: put it in God's hands, with faith and trust.[16]

God can make good come from evil when needful and
no fear of making anyone scandalized. His "instrument,"
Nebuchadnezzar, is going to besiege the city of God in
597, and carry off a section of the population. Ten years
later, he will return. The year 587 marks the end of
Jerusalem, after a terrible siege, and of the kingdom of
Judah, the end—to all appearances—of God's people.

This ordeal God will no doubt have spared Habakkuk,
but he will put Jeremiah through it and entrust the last-
named with bringing it home to his people.

JEREMIAH

> "Without this extraordinary being, the
> religious history of mankind would have
> taken another course. . . . There would
> have been no Christianity."
>
> Renan

"Some say you are Jeremiah" (Matt. 16:14). In many regards, Jeremiah is the type of the Christ: "the prophet who suffered most," living in strict communion with his God, rejected by his people; his proclamation of the new covenant will be explicitly made real by Christ the night of the Last Supper. Especially, perhaps, is their work identical: what the one accomplished for his people, the other had prepared, making it live in advance in terms of sacrament to this people. Had he not done so, could Christ have made it real? Had he not written it, would we have been able to grasp what Christ wanted to make real?

Christ, in him, brought humanity from death to life.

The death which faced the Jewish people at the time of the exile, far from being annihilating, became, thanks to Jeremiah, a way to the true life.

The message of Jeremiah was therefore closely bound up with political reality.[17] 2 Kings 21-25 gives the historical background.

"Yahweh has rejected them" (Jer. 6:30)

His first preaching (Jer. 2-6), between 626 and 622 B.C., differs scarcely at all from his predecessors: Amos; Isaiah; and in particular, Hosea.

2:1-3:5, general note: Judgment and condemnation. A key word, the people have **abandoned** God.

3:1-5 may seem to indicate the situation is not remediable.

3:6; 4:4, on the other hand, sees the possibility of repentance. The key word, **return.**

4:5-31, "Prophet to destroy . . . ." Jeremiah inveighs against the north, the enemy at the gate.

5:6, the root causes of the invasion? Lack of faith and lack of obedience.

6:27-30 summarized their woeful predicament.

After 622 B.C. "discovery of Deuteronomy" (see p. 65), and reform of Josiah soon shunned. Jeremiah silent.

From 605 (rise of Nebuchadnezzar), the prophet in his prime. Also, the period of his Calvary.

(The chronological order of the oracles of Jeremiah was not followed in his book; see the introduction in the Jerusalem Bible, p. 1127. Impossible to give a commentary, but some signposts may be useful to guide you in regard to further reading.)

"Long live the French revolution!"

Paradox of Christianity and, first, of Christ. God is invisible. To be known, he makes himself man, and visible, in his Son. Now the Son will refuse to tell the crowds in so many words that he is God visible, until death has destroyed the visible body. So great did he deem the danger, lest we go no further than the carnal body, the accessory, halting at the "carnal body" of the Church, the temporal incarnation and wealth. Revolutions and persecutions necessary, to make the temporal aspect keep on dying the death, the indispensable aspect of Church and Christians alike leading back to the essential.

Jeremiah gives us a pattern for what the Church, and each of us in the Church, must keep on doing and redoing (with the help of government).

The Jewish religion was linked to the temple (wanted by David), the Ark of the Covenant (the covenant given to Moses by God), sacrifices and the law, circumcision (the carnal sign that the faith of Abraham consecrated). But for the people, all this had become the essential, safeguards even in the face of God. For them to become once more signs of the essential, there must disappear:

● the Ark of the Covenant (3:16);

● fetish temple (and our parishes, turn and turn about) (7:1-15; 26; see Matt. 21:12-13; 24:1-2; 26:60; Acts 6:13-14);

● circumcision of the flesh (our sacraments and Sunday Mass, a bit of insurance for the world to come) (4:4; 9:24-25; see Rom. 2:28-29);

● Jerusalem (or our pride as Christians) (19; cf. Matt. 24:2).

Necessary purifications. Salutary, provided that in destroying the accessory they do not remove the essential along with it. Indispensable role of the prophet (in all ages): it is his job to make the distinction plain in the spirit to those whom God purifies by this means.

Destroying religion in the official sense, Jeremiah wanted to get at the true sense: religion must be from the heart. He lived this, before teaching about it.

"Religion from the heart" lived by Jeremiah.

His "confessions"

Dis-incarnate thinking is wearing. To get through to us, the truth has got to be lived, to come to us by means of another man. That is why Jeremiah wants our attention: his "confessions" are startling. Jeremiah had suffered in the flesh what he pronounced. It makes impressive reading to see how God sets about training a "militant."

In the "night of darkness" (15:10-21), Jeremiah knows that a vocation does not mean saying Yes once and for all; rather, it depends upon faithfulness. God has to keep on recalling us to what it is that unifies our lives.

12:1-5, a real outburst. Jeremiah asks God something he just cannot understand: why the wicked do well and he—Jeremiah—suffers when he is on God's side. God's answer is disconcerting, if a word of comfort was expected. God hardens his heart; there is a touch of irony, of "more to come." With Job, God goes into some detail before delivering the knockout blow. Here (and how much more moving) God is so sure of Jeremiah's love that he refuses to countenance passing doubt (with the risk of Jeremiah's becoming bogged down); instead, God replies on the profound level of his pristine love (the same behavior with John the Baptist, see Matt. 11:6). When we feel discouraged, if God trusts us so far as to propose by way of consolation a bit more suffering, then may it be granted us to thank him for believing, more than we do, in the reality of our poor love!

20:7-13, lastly Jeremiah passes from blasphemy to the infinite peace of abandonment in the arms of God; feeling, first, like an outraged girl ("You have seduced me," 20:7) and then like a once-forsaken child now clutched to his father's heart (20:13).

This experience of religion crops up again in the psalms. Prayer of that kind existed long before; what is undeniable is that Jeremiah worked to give it a more personal character. His message also influenced directly a number of psalms.[18]

The incarnation of his message needs following right through the life of Jeremiah, especially the period between the two sieges of Jerusalem, 597-587 B.C. Readers may like to do this for themselves, using his teaching to guide them on the way.

Religion from the heart, taught by Jeremiah

> "I have loved you with an everlasting love," God says.

Jeremiah's message lives throughout the book, but there is a kind of summary in chapters 30-31.

Punishment now imminent (30:1-5) has a single purpose, to bring about the return of the people to God (30:10-11). But there is no return possible for the prodigal son (30:12-17, sin marks him as a leopard is marked by his spots; cf. 13:20-27). Return can only be on the Good Shepherd's shoulders (30:18-22; "I will let him come freely into my presence and he can come close to me," 30:21). The undefiled love of God leads us back to him because he loves us, because he is our Father (31:1-14). But the child, returned to the flock and repentant, is backsliding. God holds his hand; he ought to set about destroying but his love wins the day, overpowering all other considerations.

> Is Ephraim, then, so dear a son to me,
> a child so favoured,
> that after each threat of mine
> I must still remember him,
> still be deeply moved for him,
> and let my tenderness yearn over him?
>
> Jer. 31:20

"The sovereign dignity of man is being someone for whom God's heart trembles" (A. Aeschimann).[19]

31:21-22 uses imagery (concerning the resumption of loving relationship between God and his people); while 31:31-34 represents the spiritual crown of the book, explaning how it is to come about. God will re-create the covenant; it "will be different this time because the people will have become different" (Aeschimann).

No more can be said of religion from the heart, in spirit and in truth. Only one thing Jeremiah does not know: when it is going to take place.

For himself, dying in exile after the apparent failure of his whole life's work, it must just be "later."

For us, it is real because the Son of God, taking our wine in his hands, said, "This cup is the new covenant in my blood. . . . Do this in remembrance of me."

LAMENTATIONS
"durch Leiden zum Freude"

Undoubtedly composed by some escapees from the disaster of 587 B.C., attempting a poor* liturgy[20] in the ruins of the temple. These prayers "have fixed and oriented the spiritual attitude of Israel faced with the worst disaster in its history.

"The admirable themes of trust and repentance, associated with the constant line of thought of the prophets but stated here with a measure of slowness, comprise the book's lasting value and make it perpetual food for religious souls.

"The symbolical usage made thereof by the Church in Holy Week to comment on the Crucifixion bears this out. To accede to the joy of the resurrection, the way lies through the suffering of the Cross, according to the phrase of Beethoven, **durch Leiden zum Freude**" [Through suffering to joy] (A. Gelin, Introduction, in the Jerusalem Bible issued in separate parts).

[1]Archeology of the Bible, it appears, is busy happily proving that what the Bible says is true, with evidence dredged from the sands. Of Joshua's Jericho, the archeologist's pick has unfortunately found nothing, erosion having got there first. From the dig at Ai comes the information that this township so bravely taken by Joshua had been, at that period, in ruins 1,200 years old! Archeology of the Bible is in full swing, but trust your atlas (or the excellent *Cahiers on Biblical Archeology* from A. Parrot published by Delachaux & Niestlé, rather than works the intention of which is better than the outcome).

[2]With regard to Joshua stopping the sun, refer to the notes above on miracle in the Bible. The point bears repetition: trying to make everything harmonize means in the end missing the religious meaning. The text in effect does not signify that the sun materially stopped but that God miraculously intervened. Israel had neither the strength nor the time needed to win. They won. How better express it than as the "longest day of the year."

[3]Scholars may shudder, but I hope they will forgive so crude a statement of some of the formulations so scrupulously documented and ceaselessly proposed.

[4]By Yahwist (whether one man or more) is usually meant the supposed author of the tradition calling God, Yahweh.

A century later (?), but this time in the northern kingdom, another history saw the light of day: the Elohist tradition. It does not go back to the earliest times but, on the other hand, it does carry the story down to the people's arrival in the Promised Land. Less imagist than the Yahweh tradition (it avoids describing God in human guise), more learned, the Elohist evidences awareness of the moral process (God slowly educating his people, compare for instance two accounts of the same story, Gen. 12:10-20 and

Gen. 20), and great care to safeguard the transcendence of God: God seldom communicating directly anymore, but through the intermediary of dreams.

For comparing these different traditions, the following title will be most serviceable: D. Sesboué, *Les traditions bibliques* ("Biblical Traditions"), no. 11 in the series issued by the Catholic League of the Gospel.

[5]The Yahwist was not aware of it, but one day St. Paul would tell us that this spontaneity of being God's children would be ours again when God's Son born of the line of Abraham made meaningful for mankind the lost word "Father" (Gal. 3:15-18).

[6]In all, the first eleven chapters of Genesis are his, barring some Priestly additions made about five hundred years later, the most important being chapter 1, referred to again later (see pp. 103ff.).

[7]This is evidently the formalist cult where the heart is not in it, the service which one attends since he dare not throw tradition overboard or solemn Communion carried out for the sake of being able to be married in Church.

[8]This means the invention of the sacraments. In the broad sense, a sacrament is something we know well and which betokens for us the sign of the invisible. In a precise sense, it means the seven signs which in the Church not only make something understood but make real what they represent.

[9]Sacrament of repentance and source of joy. If we come and confess, it is that God has given us grace to feel ourselves sinful and thus that he has loved us and that we have let ourselves be loved enough by him for him to forgive us. Joy of letting God make manifest toward us the all-powerfulness of his pure love.

[10]I live by the cathedral, the street dark and narrow, has long been used as a trysting-place. I would like those young people to know how important it is for them to love well. The freshness of their love is the most moving sign of the ever-young tenderness of God. If they love ill, for me they are still a sign of my refusal of love. Sin is not lack of observance of law but like the

unfaithfulness of a wife to her husband, the refusal of the tenderness of God.

[11]Mentioning it here anticipates the literary history of Israel. But there is no better introduction to this book than the message of Hosea.

[12]For the time being we are dealing exclusively with the work of this great prophet, who was prophesying in the kingdom of Judah from 740 to 701 B.C.; this work covers roughly the first thirty-nine chapters of the book of Isaiah (except chs. 24-27 and 34-35, and some further passages). A disciple of Isaiah continued his work during the exile, to give the exiles heart (prior to 538 B.C.): Isaiah 40-55, the Book of the Consolation, sometimes called Deutero-Isaiah (see p. 109). It was eventually finished by a third follower, after the resettlement of Palestine (Isa. 56-66; see p. 118).

[13]Refer back to the remarks on visions, p. 41. Isaiah does not describe God, he only sees the invisible: he experiences God's presence.

[14]The fine short book of Micah (chs. 4-5) is doubtless post-exile. Because the suffering of exile is behind them, they know where the pride of kings leads as well as that of great men lording it in proud Jerusalem. They know that the child to be born of the "young woman" of Isa. 7, the Messiah, will be no warrior king but a simple shepherd to be born in the very small town of the simple shepherd David: Bethlehem. This will mark the beginning of the messianic age, when there will be only peace.

[15]Les pauvres de Yahvé ("The Poor Men of Yahweh") (Cerf, 1956), p. 34. The reader will find in this small book the heart of the biblical message.

[16]Referred to again later, with Job. See pp. 138ff.

[17]Something of burning topicality needs to be written about the political attitude of Jeremiah, "traitor" to his own country. He affirmed that, politically speaking (as in everything else), the lead belonged to God; this he maintained during the siege (role of the Chaldeans) and the famine (the king's doing).

"It is absolutely impossible for a Christian loving his country with a love natural and supernatural to want victory in wartime for his country, even at the expense of justice" (Statmann). The Christian cannot receive other appellations than those given to Jeremiah and to the Christ: a traitor to his own country, or apostle of peace, "depending whether our stand on the side of the law of God places us—along with justice—on the side of victor or vanquished" (K. Thieme).

[18]Subject for a book, The Psalter according to Jeremiah. The author, P. E. Bonnard, sees a direct influence in some thirty of the psalms.

[19]Le Prophète Jérémie ("The Prophet Jeremiah") by the Protestant A. Aeschimann (published by Delachaux & Niestlé) is the best commentary now available.

[20]These Lamentations are not Jeremiah's except in name. The attribution has been responsible to no little extent for the view of this prophet as the author of tales of woe, whereas in him rejoicing is everywhere, though hidden, as joy is hidden in the heart of a woman in labor.

IV

FROM SINFUL KINGDOM TO
HOLY COMMUNITY

1 **Father of the Judaic Community** (Ezekiel)

A great "baroque poet" (Steinmann)

The baroque gets on our nerves.

Le Corbusier made the point clear to us: concrete has a prayerful soul; the architectural line, pure and unadorned, has only to reveal it. Since then a church making us prayerful, giving us the sense of the presence of God, is an unadorned church like Vézelay or like Ronchamp.

But God favors the baroque. I can do nothing about it. If you ever pray at length in the churches of Austria and Bavaria, then perhaps you will see it from his point of view. The exuberance, the gilded wood, convey with as much force as the Romanesque the fascinating presence of God, "All-other" than us.

Ezekiel is a baroque prophet. A very great prophet but baroque. He can never do anything the way anyone else does. To see what kind of personage he is, read Chapter 4. Before him, others had foretold that Jerusalem would be besieged. Watch how he goes about it. Silence reigns as he says, "Take a brick and lay it in front of you; on it scratch a city, Jerusalem. You are then to besiege it, trench round it, build earthworks, pitch camps and bring up battering-rams all round (the whole played out in miniature). Then take an iron pan and place it as if it were an iron wall between you and the city. Then turn to it; it is being besieged and you are besieging it." Like a boy at a game, he makes as if to assault it. Then God says in all seriousness, "This is a sign for the house of Israel." Amos had used a dramatic phrase to explain how Israel would dwindle to a remnant like a bit of an ear" being rescued "from the lion's mouth." Ezekiel goes over the same ground, with a great rigmarole: he takes a sharp blade and uses it on head and beard, the hair that has been cut off he scatters to the winds then picks it up and sets it alight.[1]

Ezekiel's vision: the God of Isaiah depicted by Picasso

The account of his calling is a bewildering one. Isaiah in a sublime passage tells how "All-other" took him. Ezekiel means the same, but the way he puts it! If you have seen the camera at the cinema bringing to life the nightmarish picture, **Guernica**, with brush-strokes of light, then you will know it is one of those works the details of which do not cohere on the screen though each marks the mind of the viewer with an impression that is indelible.

In the account of the vision, with the help of images mined out of biblical tradition (cherubim, cloud, fire) and enriched by features drawing on Assyro-Babylonian founts concerning sacred animals,[2] Ezekiel focuses attention on the essential in slow, progressive fashion: the one on the throne, or, rather, there was "something that looked like the glory of Yahweh." In other words, he only saw fire.

But the impression within us goes deep: God is transcendent, the "All-other" before whom faces are veiled in dread. The Ineffable One. Way above the pagan gods harnessed to his chariot.

God sees everything and is everywhere, he has everything in his hands, immutable therefore (symbol of the wheels on the ground that went forward four ways, with eyes all around).

Last (or rather, most important, since it is the newest teaching of all), the covenant was not destroyed with the ending of the national kingdom, the temple and official religion: God is not bound to one place or one institution but to one people.

This brings us to some useful dates.

As foretold by Jeremiah (605), in 597 B.C. Nebuchadnezzar besieged Jerusalem. King Jehoiachin had the foresight to surrender. The inhabitants were spared their lives but ten thousand were deported. In the group of priests exiled was Ezekiel.[3] Nothing about him to demand special attention, as yet. In five years' time, he is going to be God's representative in the concentration camp.[4] In Jerusalem, ten years of madness. Despite Jeremiah, the new king revolts and asks for Egyptian aid. Nebuchadnezzar is angry. After an 18-month siege, in June-July 587 B.C.,[5] the city falls and Nebuchadnezzar "had the sons of Zedekiah slaughtered before his eyes, then put out Zedekiah's eyes and loading him with chains, carried him off to Babylon" (2 Kings 24:7). Sack of Jerusalem; the last survivors deported.

Exile in Babylon lasted 49 years (587-538 B.C.).

Such is the background to the ministry of Ezekiel. The main characteristic of prophesying is that it employs a broad spectrum, teaching us to discern in the unfolding of history, the accomplishing of God's plan, while inviting our collaboration therein with all our strength as men. The unfolding of history, apparently profane, will now yield a group of slaves on the roads to exile, where formerly there was a regular kingdom. The message of Ezekiel is to try and persuade believers to make the changeover from sinful kingdom to holy community. The date 587 marks the great divide.

597-587: Ten years of madness

Madness of a blind people. The first siege dismantled Jerusalem. "Israel has lost a battle but has not lost the war," the Jews cry.

Ten years of madness in Jerusalem. "In order to survive, come to terms with the Chaldean," Jeremiah's advice on God's behalf. But his voice is muffled in the pit of punishment.

Ten years of madness in Babylon. "Buy yourselves houses, the captivity is going to last a long time," Jeremiah advised the deportees. They sent a letter to Jerusalem to get him hanged. False prophets arise among the people with misleading talk of peace. "Like slapping plaster on a broken wall," Ezekiel's verdict, "when it needs rebuilding" (Ezek. 13). He indicates by gesture what is going to happen to the Jews; one fine morning and he will be off, his pack upon his back, through a little hole in that wall.

Ten years of senseless carousing. Ezekiel's message is one of gloom. He foretells the end is near (Ezek. 1:33). Of the oracles, there now follow two celebrated groups.

Great allegories[6]

Ezek. 15: the vine. A theme from Isaiah, now tragic.
Ezek. 16: Ezekiel (though his manner is less assured)

develops what Hosea attempted with great delicacy, in describing the covenant between God and his people as a nuptial bond.

Ezek. 16:1-59: Israel the whore loved by God, rejected;

Ezek. 16:60-63 (text perhaps post-587 B.C.), the whore ever-loved, developing through this love. A straight account of the same story, 20:1-31, 32-49; repeated in allegorical form, in terms on occasion brutal, chap. 23.

"Unripe grapes" (Ezek. 18)

Instinctively, we think in terms of the individual, me and my maker, Newman said. God thinks primarily in terms of "people" (and now, Church). He has made a covenant with a people; so the people collectively are responsible to him for the covenant and each of us only insofar as within that people enveloped in him.[7]

This feeling of collective responsibility before God[8] entailed risks: with the exile, the people collectively stood rejected. The unavoidable and despairing conclusion seemed to be that all individuals, each and every one, good and bad, were rejected.

Jeremiah had already timidly broached the principle of dissociation (Jer. 31:29). It remained for Ezekiel to provide the groundwork of theory: everyone is responsible for his own destiny; the choice of the individual for God or against him is constantly repeated.[9]

587 B.C.: Collapse

"It is nothing," the false prophets said; in secret, the deportees got the flags ready for the day their brothers came to set them free. That's how it went with the survivors, a halter round their necks, dragging themselves exhausted in the wake of their blinded king whose last sight was of his own murdered sons.

Some of them objected. "What the Lord does is unjust" (Ezek. 33:17-20).

Others despaired. "Our sins weigh heavily on us. How are we to go on living?" (Ezek. 33:10-16).

Post-587 B.C.: "Promise of future resurrections" (S. de Dietrich)

Did you ever attend the Good Friday office in a Greek church? The Latin church mourns for the death of our Lord; Byzantine liturgy loudly proclaims joyous Alleluias in a brilliantly lit, flower-filled temple, for Christ is dead and will rise again and so we are saved.

With the collapse of his people, Ezekiel understands he is come to Calvary, where the road to the Cross ends; but yonder, perhaps a long way off, there is the resurrection. Ezekiel intones his finest songs of hope in the midst of a broken people.

The shepherds and the Good Shepherd (Ezek. 34; 37:15-18)

The shepherds (kings and priests) have led the people to their downfall. God himself will take care of his flock, or, rather, he will do it by the intermediary of his servant David. Read the many references in the margins of your Bible and you will appreciate how this passage from Ezekiel deepens their meaning.

The dry bones (Ezek. 37)

The living God is the one who gives life. His people are dead.[10] God by his Word re-creates them, then by his Spirit gives them life. This extraordinary vision is one of the Old Testament's nearest approximations to the

Trinity: God (one day we shall know this to be God the Father) creates by his word the Word and gives it life by his Spirit.[11]

The new heart (Ezek. 36, esp. vss. 16-38)

One of Ezekiel's greatest achievements (marvelous setting by Honegger for the oratorio by Claudel, **Dance of Death**). At last God can be loved, for he will have torn out our stony hearts and given us hearts of flesh and blood instead, meaning hearts whence the spirit can freely cry to him, "Abba, father" (cf. Rom. 8:15). Then, God says, when I have brought you back to me and you love me, you will know what sinners you have been and will be sorry for your sins.[12] Thus, the "name of God will be sanctified."

Holy presence of God

Read, in this order Ezek. 1, then 9:3; 10:4-5, 18-22; 11:22-23; and last 43:1-12. The ground covered will be impressive. Slowly and by stages, God leaves the temple and moves east, to the place where his people are exiled. No stronger expression could be given the central idea of the Bible: God does not live materially in one place, he lives spiritually in a faithful people.

This is far more compromising. For God to live materially in one place commits you to nothing except a vase of flowers for the altar. Knowing God lives in his people, that is, in every one of us at school, at home, and at work, also in a communal sense, meaning in the Christian group at school or at work, is all very worrying. To be responsible,[13] together, to God brings down the burning touch of God's terrible holiness on our heads. "Be holy because I am holy," God said. This is the idea that gets hold of Ezekiel with all its force. He develops it in the closing chapters.

The torah of holiness (Ezek. 40-48)

This bit is difficult going. Read it through. It is from the difficulty that the religious approach desired will be formed in us, God is holy, that is to say, apart and pure. He lives in the midst of his people so they too ought to be holy, apart (especially the pagan people among whom they are presently living, "I do not pray for them to be taken from the world but keep them from ill") and pure. Since God lives in them (Yahweh-is-there, Ezekiel's last word), the whole life of the people lacks meaning except in relation to him; their life becomes worship, the service of God. Disinterestedly. The liturgical cult of the thousand minute prescriptions is only the model for what our lives should become in service, and that a poor copy of heaven (see Revelation), a passionate summons for the day when Christian people, true sons of the Son, will live forever in the eternal bliss of the Son with his Father in the Trinity.

2 Exile: The New Community Finds a Soul and Law

(A) SOUL OF THE NEW PEOPLE

As the developing bath makes plain the unknown image on the photographic plate, so the message of Ezekiel suddenly made plain to the exiles (at least to the best of them, including the priests) the image of the people of God obliterated by four centuries of surfeit and sinning.

The Remnant thus discovered what had always been their true nature, now made plain by suffering: they were a people apart, separate, "holy" because the Lord is holy (understood the more clearly now they were lost in the midst of this vast empire, with its multiple and multiform gods). The carnal body of God's presence (the temple, the Ark, and the official religion) had disappeared. As Christ went from the sight of the pilgrims at Emmaus, who were overwhelmed, and left a presence already spiritualized in his eucharistic body, in the same way Ezekiel taught his brothers in exile that this presence of God lived on amongst them by his Word, in the Word of the law given to Moses and in part written down, in the Word transmitted in burning terms by the prophets. All the love that would have gone, and indeed had gone, to the temple now went to the Word of God. Worship came to mean reading of the law, and the synagogue replaced the temple. "Judaism" was born.

Studying the law of Moses contained in the three traditions already composed (and perhaps to some extent amalgamated?) with help from oral traditions additionally, in view of new circumstances and illumined by the message of the prophets, a group of priests—understanding the better thereby what God wanted to say and do through Moses—set about completing the old accounts in order to cover all potentialities. This is what is called the Priestly tradition.[14]

Although it was no doubt finished later, the main groups will now be considered (following Ezekiel), namely, the second part of the book of Exodus, Leviticus, and Genesis chapter one.

God's real presence in his people (Exod. 25-31; 34-40)

Two parts almost identical. In the first, "God said to Moses, Do this and do that for me"; in the second, "Moses did this and he did that as God commanded." The reference is to the building of the temple (or, rather, the tent in the Wilderness, seen through the temple of Solomon). The repetition is instructive: we do not have to invent the worship we render to God but receive it at his hands. Our liturgy, St. John will be repeating, is only the terrestrial copy of that of heaven.

But—and this is the second lesson—God does not want worship from a slave people, no servile imitation. His commandment to serve him addresses itself to the heart of everyone. Note the significant repetition, those who work on building the sanctuary are "all the men and women whose heart prompted them" (or spirit); again 35:20-36:7 offers us the "admirable vision of the people of God offering and employing all means to build a holy place where God will be served worthily. Each has a place and purpose in the host of tasks and skills" (G. Auzou).

"Make me a sanctuary so that I can live amongst them" —that is the text enshrined in these pages, Exod. 25:17-22. The telephoto lens covering the temple as a whole pans slowly in the direction of the mercy-seat; the shots converge on a sole location, the empty space upon the throne between the two cherubim. The heart of Israel is beating there; once yearly, that is where the blood of the atonement is to be shed (see Lev. 16); and that is where God "mysterium tremendum et fascinans" makes his presence felt, meeting man.[15]

The one place the whole world over where God makes his presence felt. Paul recalled this, telling us in a collective formula that the body of Christ is both the home of God's real presence on earth and the one by whose blood we have access to God ("No one can see God and survive";

Christ died shedding his blood upon the Mercy-seat which is his body). His words will be, that Christ Jesus "was appointed by God to sacrifice his life" (Rom. 3:25).

LEVITICUS

"Nothing but blood and sexual taboos: what a dreadful book." Add rubrics of painstaking detail but colorless, a boring style made up of endless repetition, and there you have the book of Leviticus.

A marvelous book.

The Holy One does not show himself or his power. He works through the attitude of another, or may be glimpsed therefrom. An unbeliever is not going to see into the heart of the mystery by staring at a consecrated Host but by observing the infinite respect and love with which the Host is surrounded by those who believe Jesus present there.

Leviticus describes the attitude of those who serve the Lord (with rites perhaps outmoded) and brings us to the presence of the living God, conveying to us that his service is a mystery of communion.

Presence of God

God named in every paragraph (more than 350 times!).

He is the Holy One, All-other, the One to whom everything belongs because he is the Lord. We may have the usage but he can consecrate everything to himself. He is the one who can demand a people or man of this people have nothing on this earth but himself.

He is the living One, meaning he has within himself a potentiality such that those who have drawn near to him are unable to express it, except by a feeling of dread before the Holy One.

The people feel they live in God's presence (before Yahweh": 55 times!) They live thus, body and soul. To enter into communion with God, inner contemplation is not sufficient (it often leads to neglect of outward things). A man prays with his whole body.[16] This is what the rubrics mean. But time is required, and time is necessary to get on terms with what is holy, to "make ready the heart." Their final aim is to prepare us for the inner sacrifice and express it.

The people live in a world where everything speaks of God, where everything is a sign from God who made it (Leviticus, an excellent introduction to the sacraments).

The people feel God living in them. Welling up from within, the people sense something of the extraordinary potentiality of the God of life and are terrified. Hence the precise rules and regulations governing blood and sex relations.

Blood: for a Semite, it means life (when blood is shed, for example in wartime, life ebbs). Now life is the incommunicable property of God. Blood is the property of God. The prohibition concerning blood is very far from a good cooking-aid (keep off unhealthy mixtures!); it signifies awareness that only God is living and that something of his life courses in our veins and those of our brethren.

There is also the impressive feeling of participating in the work of God, in the mystery of fatherhood and of motherhood, and this gives all that has to do with sex its sacred aspect.

Last, because God is a mystery that fascinates:

Leviticus is a call to consecrate oneself to God. This

call re-echoes in the heart of every Christian consecrated to God in baptism.

On occasion, the call is so pressing that the man who hears it understands he can no longer live—even here below—for any other than for God. "The moment I believed there was a God," Father de Foucauld wrote, "I understood I could do nothing else but live only for him. . . . God is so great, so wide the difference between God and all else." Leviticus and the book of Numbers (Num. 1-10) continuing it, they are the place to which all those who have consecrated themselves to God, in seclusion or in the world, ought to keep returning in order to understand the meaning of their lives: through them,[17] we "see" that everything belongs to God and, thus, that we should receive our lives as a gift of God. Lastly, it is because they are "given" to God, freely, in "pure loss" that God grants us the usage of this world which belongs to him.[18]

GENESIS, CHAPTER 1

Cosmic liturgy

All these themes, a great poet was to take up in the best- (and least-) known Old Testament passage: the first account of the creation.

A note on the historical background. The scene is set in Babylon; the exiles would have been familiar with the old cosmogonies, fifteen centuries of tradition behind them. The widest currency went to the epic battle between the god Marduk and goddess Tiamat; Marduk won and opened her in two like an oyster, making the firmament of heaven out of the one half and the earth out of the other. The outlook of the Mesopotamians would also have become known to them: pessimist, with men seen merely as the playthings of the gods who were sinful and irascible, wreaking their hatreds on the heads of humankind. The elements were feared (frequent flooding, unlike the Nile, had disastrous consequences; the Deluge recollects a terrifying occasion). Sacrifices were made to the sun god and moon goddess to placate these powers.

Moreover, the Jewish priesthood shorn of their rites of worship began to understand that the whole world offers worship to God[19] and that observing the Sabbath (as ordained in the Decalogue, see Exod. 20:8) aims solely at making us consecrate time to God.

Perhaps springing from the extraordinary vision wherein Ezekiel contemplated God re-creating his people by his all-powerful Word and giving them life again by his Spirit (Ezek. 37), the priest-author created this commanding gateway to the Bible as we know it:

"In the beginning God created the heavens and earth."

The statement is, first, metaphysical: before the earth (is God creating or organizing it?), before the abyss (the Hebrew word for which is strangely reminiscent of the name of the goddess Tiamat), God was. God and his Spirit floating on the waters, God and his Word: Yahweh said, etc.

Now at God's Word the toilworn maleficent world of the pagans takes on magnificent processional order: light, heaven, the waters and the earth, then the "two lamps of the holy sacrament" (sun and moon not referred to by name, since they were Babylonian gods, but as "luminaries," which is the word the priests use elsewhere for the lamps of the sanctuary: the universe is therefore a temple!), living creatures and last to arrive in this magnificent temple of creation, last because worthiest, the priest of this rite of worship: man. Not the scared, fearful mortal of ancient mythologies, but man the "image of God." Man who, working in community (note that the "image of God" is not man or woman, but man and woman, in the happy union of love), ought to raise from the world of the material the hidden image of God.

The seventh day, God rested (literally, "made the Sabbath").

This is the key to the way creation was spread over the six days:[20] God worked in the image of our week to teach us to stop at his image. Part of our time (Sunday, the Christian Sabbath) is consecrated to God. God knows the joy there is in creating the world. He also knows we run the danger, wrapped in doing, of seeing no further than outward appearances and thus producing work that is only profane. One day in seven is consecrated to him and makes us pause so that in silence we can hear the world's soul beating, while in us the "spiritual energy" finds release which draws the world to its end purpose. This consecrated moment allows men to awake to the "sense of the close bond linking all the movements of this world in the unique work of the Incarnation." Then they can no longer "give themselves to a single one of their tasks without illuminating it with the clear vision that their work—however elementary it may be—is received and made use of by a Centre of the universe."[21]

Our four accounts of the history of the people of God have now been composed.

As the account of their infancy becomes more and more meaningful in proportion as life reveals new potentialities, so the revelation of God to Moses, always the same revelation, in the course of a thousand years has

revealed more and more clearly the plan of love God
entrusted to his friend.

It was tempting at this stage to go over the account—
or rather the accounts—again, to stress this plan of God's.

Who made the attempt? Was it Ezra, the scribe who
will read this law solemnly in Jerusalem in the year 428
B.C.? Was it another person, or persons, before him?
Whoever he was, the theology of Ezekiel as experienced
in Priestly circles during the captivity, roused in his heart
a lasting echo.

The four laws in one: The Hexateuch

Consider the diagram below;[22] it will help you weave
your way through this wondrous composition.

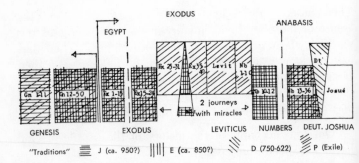

(B) LAW OF THE NEW PEOPLE

The second part unifies five books: Exodus, Leviticus, Numbers, Deuteronomy, and Joshua. Three main happenings may be distinguished:

Two main parts:

The first comprises Genesis. Holy history with a successful outcome: dealing with men, who are at times sinners but whose relationship with God is based on love. God loves Abraham, Isaac, Jacob, Joseph, and they trust in him. There is no law, no contract between them except the unilateral arrangement of the covenant, God's promise to lead them to well-being. Prefiguration of what would one day become of this dialogue when mankind in Christ Jesus will be able to call God "Our Father."

Then came sin. The bondage of sin. Slavery in Egypt. When things are at their very worst (Is that a law of history? See the captivity, the death of Christ and the day of doom with its attendant cataclysmic disasters), God takes a hand.

In Egypt: Exod. 1-15. Egypt standing for the servitude of sin. Man is alienated, sunken in historical events from which God alone can deliver him. Pharaoh is powerless in that his empire is voracious and, to keep going, slave-labor is essential; the bosses can do nothing since capital consumes itself and always wants more. Only God by a lightning stroke like the Passover, by slow action like that of the Christians incarnating the doctrine of the Church, can free mankind.

Exodus. A journey through the Wilderness, a journey marked by miracles, brings us first to Sinai where God makes the covenant, from there to Kadesh where the people stop over for the space of one generation. Between the two stages, making explicit the thought of Moses,

Priestly law comes into being (Exod. 25-40; Lev.; Num. 1-10). Following Moses, flight from Egypt, marching to the Promised Land. "From slavery to service,"[23] from this oppressed class kept together by ancestral memories, God is going to make a people on the move, a community of brothers communing with one another in serving God with love, serving him with rites of worship (Exod. 25-40; Lev.) which summarize and most especially symbolize the service, the sacrament: a community which will make its life, prayer, and action one of worship.

The Anabasis. From Num. 13 (there is a gap of thirty-eight years between the last verse of Num. 12 and the first verse of Num. 13), we are well on the way to the Promised Land. Following Joshua ("Yahweh-saves") like a tidal wave to the kingdom where all the tribes of the Chosen People will consecrate themselves to God by the Shechem pact (Josh. 24) and, tasting the marvelous fruits of the land of Canaan, will serve God according to the new charter of Deuteronomy; a tidal wave to the lasting Kingdom, to which we come by Jesus ("Yahweh-saves") with love for our charter and for nourishment—as well as manna and indeed the Eucharist, there is the eternal communion of mankind and the universe animated by the Spirit, with God in Christ Jesus.

3   Home from Captivity: The Community at Grips with Reality

Coming out of the cinema, or, back down-to-earth

Did you ever feel sad coming out of the cinema after a film? End of make-believe and high adventure. Back to work, school, friends. Back to one's self. Impossible to go on identifying with the star, male or female. A wonderful time and then back to reality, true life goes on.

True life for the Jewish people lay in the captivity: marvelous hours spent living again the glorious deeds of the past; return to reality: it is the captivity, with no king (well, Jehoiachin is still in prison), no homeland, no temple. Exactly as a thousand years earlier when they were enslaved in Egypt.

Exactly as a thousand year earlier in Egypt? Well then, nothing has been lost. Perhaps the film is what is real, true life? God is still Yahweh, his name is still Yahweh-who-brought-us-out-of-the-house-of-bondage. Yahweh can still get us out of slavery now, can still raise up a liberator, open up a way through the wilderness and carry us back to the land of our forefathers.

> "Console my people, console them"
> says your God.
> "Speak to the heart of Jerusalem
> and call to her
> that her time of service is ended,
> that her sin is atoned for."
> Isa. 40:1-2

Toward the end of the captivity, this strange certainty took hold of the heart of a disciple of Isaiah's (scholars refer to him as Deutero-Isaiah); he understood that the voice he could hear in his heart was that of God himself.

CONSOLATION OF ISRAEL
(Isa. 40-54)[24]

The priestly history is a meditation on the exodus to discover its depth of meaning and adore therein God's handiwork.

These fifteen chapters also come as a meditation in lyrical style on the exodus. The only thing is that the aim is not adoring God in past history but, rather, making him take action in the present by a reminder of past deeds of his. Certain compliments get things done quicker than demands do, owing to the person at the receiving end having to live up to the reputation.

Have a look at the map. We are in Babylon. Nabonidus has succeeded Nebuchadnezzar. A mystic, he restores the temple of the gods. Soon he will retire for a period of seven years (why so?) into the remote desert, leaving the reins of power in the hands of his son Belsharusur (Belshazzar of the Bible). The rise of a new kingdom on the eastern confines of the empire rouses small concern.

"Let us leave the little Median kings to be beaten by a little Persian king: the Babylonian empire is solid and unified from the Persian Gulf to the Red Sea, the Fertile Crescent has a natural defense barrier in the impenetrable wastelands of Arabia."

But the little king was Cyrus, and he will conquer the world. Cyrus, a good king. Loved by his subjects. Loved by his enemies, subjects-to-be.

For Second Isaiah, Cyrus is the messiah, the one God has taken by the right hand to liberate his people by means of him.

You know enough now to speed along through these chapters.

One intuition enlivens them from start to finish: God is going to start another exodus. He is going to set his people free. This will be so marvelous that the people will have no time to go the long way round, the usual and only way along the Fertile Crescent. God is going to open up a highway straight through the trackless desert. From Babylon to Jerusalem, a thousand kilometers of sand

and volcanic rock. No, a thousand kilometers through green pastures and by running waters.[25]

This unique intuition is orchestrated on three basic themes:

• This liberation is possible because God is what he is, the only God. The only one who is able to create and to see into the future. The only one, before whom the other gods of the heathen are as nothing (see notes, Isa. 42:8; 41:21).

• This God is not—as was perhaps formerly held—only or especially the God of a people Israel; he is the universal Lord of all peoples (note, Isa. 45:14);

• Israel is the servant of God, charged with a mission in this world (it remains the same for the Church and for each of us in the Church): to be the "light of the nations," to bear witness to other peoples of the true God (notes, Isa. 41:8; 43:10).

The future is bright. God loves his people![26] Forget the past: God is going to start afresh!

But, the future is going to be dreadful . . .

Writing on the wall in Babylon

On a summer morning in the year 538 B.C., the department in charge of municipal affairs posted the new edict of Cyrus the Great on the walls of Babylon; it has just received his signature at the summer palace in Ecbatana, miles away.

"Thus speaks Cyrus king of Persia, Yahweh god of heaven had given me all the kingdoms of the earth! Whoever there is among you of all his people, may his God be with him! Let him go up to Jerusalem in Judah to build the temple of Yahweh, god of Israel" (Ezra 1:3).[27]

This is the Cyrus of the history books, who the previous year had made a sensational entry into Babylon.

Belshazzar's feast, or the uninvited guest

Nabonidus and his son Belshazzar were bored. There had been a stir, the first day they saw strange earthworks being thrown up below the ramparts; in charge was Cyrus, whom they thought to be 2,000 kilometers away in Asia Minor; shortly before, in 546 B.C., he had entered Sardis and ransacked the fabled treasures of Croesus. Since then, it was all very dull, the siege endless. The walls of Babylon were stout and the reserves immense. Nothing to fear. But amusements were getting hard to come by. Hunting was at an end. Nothing to do but eat.

Belshazzar invited his noblemen to the palace. The sacred vessels looted from the temple in Jerusalem were used to drink the health of poor King Cyrus wearing himself out below the impregnable walls, to no purpose. If they had thought, they could have invited him. The king's cup dropped from his nerveless hands: the uninvited Cyrus was there—he had just come in!

The river, running through the city, dried up overnight and enabled him to penetrate the citadel and take it without a blow exchanged.[28]

No bloodshed later, either. Cyrus, unlike the Assyrian or Babylonian kings, was praiseworthy. Loved by his subjects to whom he was a father, he only wished his conquered subjects to love him too. One of his first acts when he got control of the empire was to liberate the deportees. For the Jewish nation, he went as far as paying indemnity.

A way through the wilderness

Joy without parallel in the Jewish quarters of Babylon! Some would doubtless opt to stay rich in exile. But the faithful under the leadership of Sheshbazzar started the trek home. Second Isaiah had told the truth, Yahweh was come for his people. A second exodus began to the Promised Land where a future was in store for them that King Solomon himself might have envied. What festivities on getting back to the land of their forefathers!

But who among them had ever heard of a land remaining unoccupied for fifty years? The Jews got home and found their fields tilled and their houses lived in by folk who could scarcely be brought to believe they had not always been the owners. So the troubles started. Other troubles followed, from outside sources: the Samaritans were not pleased at the prospect of hotheads from Judah resettling, and although there was no preventing them holding solemn festivities to mark the resumption of worship on the temple site, they resorted to any means —threats, chicanery and denunciation—to make it impossible for them to start building the temple all over again. And they succeeded. Even the best of the newly returned grew downhearted. It was not just squabbling with the squatters, lack of government supervision, Samaritan opposition, there was also the problem of food-gathering. A corner of land had to be taken as and where it could be found, then its cultivation, and the building of a dwelling-house. To crown it all, the father-figure of Cyrus was succeeded by the tyrant Cambyses and he was to conquer Egypt, the route to conquest passing through a Palestine already exhaused by a series of bad harvests.

"The wilderness will blossom." How ironical the magnificent promises now sounded.

Why is the lover of God always humiliated and persecuted?

"The wilderness will blossom." O Lord, you have deceived us. They were all very well, those fine promises by the mouth of your prophet. Those of us who did not wish to believe them are happy now and well-off in Babylon. And we your faithful servants are here, hungry, humiliated, hounded.

One man was especially to blame for letting down a whole people, the one who transmitted the promises (or his close disciple). One thing was certain; God inspired them. So they turned back to the texts and meditated on the oracles to try and understand the real meaning of them.

God chose his people to serve him, to bear witness for him to all nations. How could such a servant accomplish such a mission through suffering, with all this humiliation and persecution? Why, when one behaves like a Christian, at school or work, must one be cold-shouldered? And if it is a matter of course for the lover of God to be persecuted always, how can God make him "bear fruit" in spite of his powerlessness?

One day God gave the prophet to understand this: he does not save us **despite** suffering and the death of his servants but **through** them. Straightway, the prophet wrote the Songs of the Suffering Servant. Then, because these songs were the key to all his work, he skillfully worked them into the second part of Isaiah, to shed light on the true meaning thereof.

THE SONGS OF THE SUFFERING SERVANT

(Isa. 42:1-9; 49:1-6; 50:4-11; 52:13-53:12)

God's people are his servant: this is the servant whom

the disciple of Isaiah was writing about. Mindful of the great ones who had been persecuted in the past, Moses and Jeremiah in particular, he sees them humiliated in Babylon and humiliated in Palestine. The people personified (at times so highly, the figure becomes distinct from the people themselves, as Christ one day would stand for mankind but distinct enough from them to save them), the people are called by God to transmit the "light to the nations" not by force as was believed but by faith in God (first and second songs). The mission was a sorrowful one; the third song tells how the servant bore his suffering, abandoned in God's hands. It represents a peak in the Old Testament; beyond it, nothing more to expect but beholding what he foretells come to pass: the servant who suffers and dies . . . for others. With this poem, the people's suffering takes on meaning; it is no longer a curse, but their redemption.

When the first Christians recognize the Suffering Servant in the man who was crucified and rose again from the dead (see Acts 3:22; Luke 2:32), they will recognize that they are saved because in him are the whole people whom he personifies, once dead and now living through God.

But for the time being, something much more prosaic is happening: it is a question of survival, and the going is hard. Life of God's people, the image of each of our lives: setting out with enthusiasm to conquer the world and evangelize it, the dullness of everyday life and its demands quickly serve to disillusion us. Such was the Remnant of Israel, bearers of God's promise, busy building themselves houses to live in, sweeping up, struggling with poor harvests. The temple, the home and sign of God's presence, there was no one to see to it.

Fortunately, God does not leave us for long undisturbed. About the year 520 B.C., two prophets arose: Haggai and Zechariah.[29]

HAGGAI

In cutting language, Haggai lodges his protest: "Is this a time for you to live in your panelled houses, when this House [the temple] lies in ruins. That is why everything is going wrong."

Besides the abandonment of the temple, the people's attitude was the root cause. "It was no less a question than deciding if Israel was going to rebuild its national life with or without God" (Dietrich). When a people, when the faithful in Christ, put their own creature comforts before the adoration of their Lord, then God can no longer be with them.

The message of Haggai was listened to and the people got down to the job: in 515 B.C., the solemn consecration of the second temple. The old men who had seen the splendor of Solomon's temple no doubt wept at the poverty of this one. But, Haggai proclaimed, it is in this one that God is going to give peace (Hag. 2:9). In the shadow of this temple, restored by Herod, the risen Christ will declare to his apostles, "My peace I give unto you."

4 The Passover of 515 B.C.: Birth of Judaism

There are dates in history commonly regarded as turning points, whether in civilizations or the ebb and flow of power. The year 515 was such a date.

For four hundred years Israel had been a kingdom, from the time David had made Jerusalem his capital in the year 1,000 B.C. It was a nation the sun shone on, with king and court, a temple with complex sacrificial liturgy, and an unceasing line of prophets who proclaimed stand-ards of behavior. God allowed or wanted all of this. The only thing was that to his way of thinking, it was no more than a prefiguration of the lasting spiritual Kingdom. And Israel thought it was already with them! They had mis-taken the means for the end. The substance no longer attracted them, as they had the shadow: history was at an impasse. To get things moving again, God found no other means but to destroy the shadow.

Exile in Babylon.

Refined by fifty years of suffering, Israel was back home again. But the political kingdom was finished for-evermore. There was no longer a king; the temple was a shambles. The end of independence: to the Persian tutelage, there succeeded the tutelage or oppression ac-cording to the instance of the Greeks, the Ptolemies, the Seleucids, and then the Romans. Israel had become a community of poor men, whose only riches lay in the Word of God which in earlier days had been transmitted to them by the prophets (few and far between by that time) and, firstly, by the first of these prophets, Moses. A community regulated by priests whose "sacrifices" were the reading of the law. And the people's offering, before the oblations of bulls, will be that of a lowly and contrite heart. For five centuries, poor indeed in human reckoning. Five centuries of capital importance, at the end of which the People of God will bring forth the One who is to be their true king, meek and lowly: Christ Jesus.

515 B.C., a turning point in the history of Israel. Or more precisely, the resettlement in Palestine; 515 marks an important moment, continued by the work of restora-tion accomplished by Nehemiah and Ezra from 445 to 428 B.C.

What would the work of restoration amount to, when the people no longer believed in their destiny? It was to give them back their faith in their mission; over these difficult years, a disciple (or was it disciples?) of Isaiah consecrated himself to this task. His work forms chapters 55 to 66 in the book of Isaiah. It is sometimes called Trito-Isaiah.[30]

THIRD ISAIAH 56-66

"Jerusalem, lift up your head. Look at the immense crowds of those who build and those who seek. All over the world, men are toiling—in laboratories, in studios, in deserts, in factories, in the vast social crucible. The ferment that is taking place by their instrumentality in art and science and thought is happening for your sake" (Teilhard de Chardin, **The Divine Milieu, op. cit.,** p. 138).

This paradoxical message that Teilhard addressed to the Jerusalem of the twentieth century, to the Church at a time when in human matters there seems to be a falling back on all fronts, this is at root the message given the little community by Third Isaiah:

> Arise, shine out, for your light has come
> above you the glory of your God now rises
> Lift up your eyes and look round,
> The nations come to your light.

The Church's eternal paradox: the poorer in human terms, the better there shines through the Church the light making her all-radiant within and the celestial and definitive Kingdom of which she is the beginning.

Third Isaiah: a fine Gothic arch, with chapter 61, the oracle of the messenger announcing the coming of messianic times, forming the keystone.[31]

God comes to wreak vengeance on his enemies, those within and those without: all those who will not turn away from sinning and toward himself, God their Father.

God comes especially to accomplish the redemption for Zion, that is to say, the tiny Remnant of those who turn toward him, Jews and non-Jews. This Zion is described as being that much the more marvelous as the current situation grows more depressing.

So magnificent does this community of the faithful become in the mind of the poet that soon it appears before his astonished eyes like a marvelous lady beloved by God, who takes her for his wife and to whom all nations bring their gifts that they may benefit by her riches (St. Matthew remembered this when he wrote about the coming of the Magi); like a mother, bearing a new people. The redemption vouchsafed by God will not therefore be brought about without our participation.

It is thus understandable that Jesus preaching in the synagogue at Nazareth was able to bring home his mission, to identify himself with this messenger in Isa. 61: "This text is being fulfilled today even as you listen" (Luke 4:21). The New Testament will never tire of meditating on this poem in which it is announced that the Church, the promised bride purified by Christ, will in the course of ages give birth and bear the mystic body of Christ (Rev. 12), the Church of whom the Virgin Mary is the figure.

Before becoming the Church, this little community must reorganize. Two men worked at this task.

NEHEMIAH AND EZRA

The restoration work done by these two men is as important as it is involved.[32] The books that bear their names, composed of their memoirs and various documents, do not always follow chronological order.

On this April day in the year 446, in Babylon, King Artaxerxes' cupbearer, a Jew by the name of Nehemiah, is downcast. A relative has arrived from Jerusalem. The picture he has drawn of the material situation there is a gloomy one. The king is put out, since his cupbearer is not usually sad and because he is fond of him (and has to keep in with him too, being a person of importance, since the one who pours the king's cup may one day pour . . . poison). Therefore, the king gives Nehemiah leave of absence for a twelve-year period to go and rebuild the walls of the Holy City. His mission was not accomplished without difficulty. But since this excellent man does not err on the side of modesty (read, in order, Neh. 1-7:5; 11-12), the principal phases of the reconstruction of the walls are described for us and especially the admirably orchestrated celebration for the dedication of the walls. His apologia comes to an end and he returns to Babylon.

Two years later, accompanied by his friend Ezra "minister of Jewish religious affairs" at the Persian court, Nehemiah visits Jerusalem again. He is obviously curious to see what has become of his handiwork. Alas, if the reconstructed walls are well maintained, the same does not go for the good resolutions. Nehemiah reacts vigorously. Some men would have torn out their hair in desperation. Nehemiah is one of those who would rather tear out the hair of the guilty ones and throw their furniture out of the windows: it is less painful and more effective! He tells us so with complacency (Neh. 13:4-13).

But the seventh month inaugurating the sabbatical

year is at hand. Before the people assembled in the main square, Ezra reads the law of God. This ceremony (detailed in Neh. 8-10; note the admirable prayer of Ezra on the occasion) ranks with the most important occasions in the history of Israel: it may be said to mark the official birth of Judaism, that is to say, the form taken by the Jewish religion after the captivity, a form to be preserved down to the time of Christ and on to our own. The meeting no longer takes place in the temple but in the public square; it consists not in blood sacrifices but in reading the Word of God. The synagogical rite is born.

The few months spent in Jerusalem enabled Nehemiah and Ezra to estimate the peril facing the community and how it could be reduced. The Jewish community was short on sibsidies and inhabitants but, above all, deep religious life was lacking. The priests were ill-behaved in the temple itself, Jews intermarried with local people and adopted their new relations' language and religious customs. Judaism, to endure, needed thoroughgoing reform and a sound structure, resting on minutely detailed and imperative law.

Ezra returned to Babylon and got the king to grant him a **firman,** an edict (see Ezra 7). It gave him full powers to find a solution to the three points in question: endowed with considerable grants, Ezra was able to take along with him a convoy of Israelites who had remained in Babylon until then; most important of all, he was to impose religious law in Israel as the civil law. Arriving in Jerusalem in 428, Ezra acted brutally. Profoundly religious, he stood for no shilly-shallying when it came to purity of religion: all those who had taken foreign wives were "invited" (on pain of expulsion and confiscation of their worldly goods!) to present themselves within a three-day period and report that their wives were being sent home.

A brutal job. A necessary job no doubt. In any case, Ezra's impact on Judaism was profound, as much for the religious respect he bore the Word of God with which he began the solemn reading as for the manner in which he established extremely detailed and inflexible observance of the law. And the Jews were not to be mistaken in regarding Ezra as their second founder after Moses.[33]

What is purely external obedience, if there is no inner decision to reform one's life in depth? To this decision, a prophet, who may have been named Malachi, wished to bring the people: it was at the same time in history, and was done with a great deal of delicacy and persuasive gifts.

MALACHI

The people engaged in overhauling their lives.

His book, a dialogue between God and his people, preluding the definitive dialogue: "I was hungry. . . . When, Lord, have we seen you hungry?"

"I have loved you, God says. And you say, How have you loved us?" And you say . . . And you say. Eight times this refrain—what a nation of talkers! Eight times, to lay bare the sin carefully shelved out of reach of the conscious:

● sin of those who offer God the leftovers;

● sin of the priests who no longer heed God's word, "You have caused many to stumble by your teaching";

● sin of those who send their wives away. One of the finest meditations on marriage, the union of two beings both born of the unique love of God, and become a single being in themselves destined for offspring given by God;

- sin of those who can no longer tell good from bad;
- sin of the arrogant self-sufficient.

But once again, the love of God wins the day. "Before my day comes, that great and terrible day, I am going to send you a prophet like Elijah, who will turn the hearts of everyone back to the love of former times."

When John the Baptist appears, Luke will know that the day of God is at hand, since here is the prophet who is to announce it (Luke 1:17).

JOEL

It is to this "Day of God" also that a great prophet whose work is hard to date consecrates some striking passages. This "Day of Yahweh," Joel tells us, will be a terrible day. To give this people of agriculturalists some inkling of what he meant, he found no more telling image than that of a plague, unfortunately all too well known to them, a plague of locusts. This is the terrifying start to the "Day of Yahweh." However, God wants not the death of the sinner but his conversion. Joel's urgent poems calling us to repentance still ring out every year in our churches on Ash Wednesday (Joel 2:15-17; cf. 1:13-20; 2:12-14).

In response to the conversion he has achieved, God gives a promise.

Listen to this promise, it is an important one. When Peter on the morning of Pentecost has the job of telling the crowd that has gathered what is happening, he can only find the words of Joel to express it: "It is what the prophet Joel foretold that has come to pass" (Acts 2:17-21).

God, through Peter, is telling us, "By the coming of the Spirit, an end is coming too. You as Christians who are saved by invoking the name of the Lord Jesus, you will see the new world where there will be no more tears or death and where I, the Lord God, will be all things to all men."

The only difference: through Joel, God let it be believed he would do all there was to be done, alone and unaided, to end the old order and bring in the new. Through Peter, first of the long apostolic line, God is telling us, "The end of the old order is at hand but it is up to you Christians, in the light of my spirit, to bring this to pass."

Infinite perspectives opening in the people's hearts. For the time being, they cannot grasp the full implications. They are concerned with settling some small but tricky problems.

"Send away your foreign wives for the sake of the love owed to God," Ezra said. God was with Ezra in this, because he was well aware that the foreign wives were a risk to religion. But he was also well aware that an unbending attitude like Ezra's meant another risk, no less serious for religion: that of mistaking the means for the end, that of pharisaism. He cannot openly oppose his servant Ezra (who was taking risks himself for God's sake). Fortunately, God was not lacking a touch of homely humor: his people were told the following charming story.

RUTH

Divine Humor: "Obey but be intelligent"

"In the days of the Judges famine came to the land." In the days of the judges meant before 1000 B.C. (The author takes no chances, six hundred years before Ezra so the story cannot be connected with the reformer's work.) In the days of the judges, therefore, a man from Bethlehem—a true Israelite—was obliged to leave his hunger-stricken land. He went, as it chanced, to live in the country of Moab and his two sons married Moabite women. The story becomes gripping for the poor Jew with death in his soul who has just sent his wife away because both Nehemiah and Ezra have said, "You must not marry Moabite women." So he hangs on every word of this marvelous story with its rural charm. Surely everything will be put in order and the wives sent away when they get back to Bethlehem? Not a bit of it. Our author continues: in Bethlehem a truly pious Jew of the name of Boaz marries Ruth, the young widowed Moabitess; she bears him a son called Obed. The book modestly concludes, "He was the father of Jesse, father of David"!

A delightful story full of kindly humor meant from God for Ezra perhaps, certainly for us the Pharisees of all ages who think we love God because we have punctiliously followed our instructions. "It is all very well to be loving me," God says. "But do use your heads. Do not confuse the means with the end."

Of the same period perhaps, another masterpiece of divine humor:

JONAH
The Prophet Who Disagreed with God's Methods

So little agreeing with these methods that when God sends him eastwards to Nineveh, Jonah embarks for the west, for Gibraltar! Flight to the west, flight in the hold of a ship, flight in sleep. There is no help for it, God sent him to Nineveh and to Nineveh Jonah will go. God got a great fish to go after him and vomit him on the shore—eastwards! So Jonah will have to go there, at the same time everyone can tell it is God who is sending him.

But sending him where and what for? To Nineveh, to tell the inhabitants that God has had enough of them and is going to destroy them. Going to Nineveh meant nothing to Jonah, but his message pleased him well. To go and tell these hereditary foes of Israel that they are all going to perish: what a fine job!

Jonah went about the great city of Nineveh in all directions, rubbing his hands and crying aloud, "Only forty days more and it will all be destroyed!"

Nineveh was converted and God "relented; he did not inflict on them the disaster which he had threatened."

Jonah was very indignant at this and prayed to God, like this: "With you, it is always the same. One cannot trust in your word. I was a bit anxious something would go wrong, that you would go and forgive them in the end. That is why I did not want to come. Now it has happened, I can't stand any more. Please take away my life." God answers, "Do not be angry, I will explain to you."

Before hearing the explanation, one must first under-stand the indignation of Jonah, that is, of every Jew, every believer. For this Jonah is not Mr. Jonah, living in the days of Jeroboam; he is a storybook character in a carefully tailored plot to make us give vent to instinctive judgment and then exorcise it.[34] And if we are not, like Jonah, scandalized by God's methods, it may be that we have not yet grasped the absolute reality represented by the Word of God. So, before listening to what God has to say, we must all be Jonahs!

When God speaks, Jonah, like every believer, thinks his decisions are final. God announces that he must punish the sinner. Nineveh has sinned. If Nineveh is not destroyed, God is unjust and does not keep his word.

It would not, however, have been the first of God's predictions not to come about . . . at least, according to human ways of thinking. To take an example, recalling the marvelous announcement of the return from exile in Second Isaiah. After the actual return, which is lamentable, God had to do a bit of explaining to make Israel understand that Israel was his servant but had to serve him by suffering. This is one of the meanings of the Songs of the Suffering Servant. A particular case in which God offered a particular explanation.

In the period we are now studying, God judged it was time to give an explanation which would be valid for all cases, to state the principle. And this was what was entrusted to "Jonah."

Jonah is the Pharisee of all ages, loving God deeply and respecting his word but finding him a bit over-just by the standards of human justice. "You are saying I am not just?" the master will ask in the parable of the vineyard laborers. "Why be envious because I am generous?" (Matt. 20:1-16). We are all Pharisees; why doesn't God punish the wicked as they patently deserve? With Jonah, we cry aloud for justice. Jonah teaches us, and that is the whole basis of his message, that God is **good.** "He breaks his word, he breaks equity (men's idea of it, anyway) rather than fail in goodness and mercy toward sinners" (J. Dupont). Or better still, God explains to Jonah that his predictions of evil become effective precisely when there is no need to carry them into effect. For what God wants is not "the death of the sinner but that he may be converted and live."

At the same time, God uses the occasion to teach Jonah (and Ezra perhaps, and ourselves) his catechism and the meaning to be given certain formulas. "Outside Jerusalem, outside the Church, no salvation," it was proclaimed. That means, God declares, not that there are people outside who are not saved but that the Church must go out to all, that the Church is present everywhere a believer's heart beats, even in Nineveh, the home of corruption.

May we never forget this missionary ideal of Jonah!

[1]Ezekiel is a great classical poet also. See the oracles against Tyre and Egypt, Ezek. 27-29.

[2]What a source! Ezekiel told the pagans among whom he lived, "I know they are your gods but look, I do not disbelieve in them. These beasts have the job of drawing the chariot of my God." The animals recur, after a long process of purification through Revelation and Christian tradition, on cathedral doorways; their function is to represent the four Gospels.

[3]Some say Ezekiel was not deported until 587 and so proclaimed the first part of his message in Jerusalem, contemporaneously with Jeremiah.

[4]The term "concentration camp" is used advisedly. What was the exact situation of the deportees? The evidence is conflicting. Ps. 137 refers to suffering endured. But we also know Jews met freely in the house of their almoner. The archives of the Bank of Murashu and Sons have been retrieved by archeology from the ruins of Nippur: a number of Jews held interests. When it comes to liberation, many were none too thrilled at the idea of having to till the stony ground of Palestine again.

[5]A Babylonian chronicle recently found in a drawer at the British Museum has led some authorities to put the date one year later, in 586 B.C.

[6]This is as good a place as any to say something about two literary genres which should not be confused.

Parable, an easy way to make someone understand something he is not all that interested in knowing. For instance, Nathan was charged by God to go and tell David it was wrong to take the wife of an officer and have him murdered. A tough job. If told straight, the king would not sympathize. So Nathan recounts a bit of news, about a rich man with a thousand head of sheep who stole a poor man's one ewe lamb for the sake of a feast. A true tale? A likely one anyhow. David goes along with it and answers that the man deserves death. Nathan need only add, "But it's you."

Parable, a simple comparison (all parables ought to reduce to a comparison, In the same way, etc.). Thus, the listener anwers himself.

Allegory, a higher genre, intended more for teaching than for passing judgment (the listener is not carried along, the matter having less likelihood of truth). It is a story with a key, the characters or situations having counterparts in reality. For instance, the allegory of the vine, cf. John 16. Important distinction, not to be ignored, otherwise there is some risk of making an author (and God) mean something other than intended (cf. note on inerrancy).

For instance, the "parable" of the good samaritan. Luke means the man used charity as we ought to. Some quarters extend the allegory, and this is allowable provided it is made clear that it falls outside scriptural meaning.

Allegory: the good samaritan=Christ saving mankind, i.e., the man who fell among thieves; the hostelry=the Church; the two coins=the two commandments, etc.)

[7]Prefiguration in the Old Testament of what the New Testament is going to reveal to us: God loves us in his Son. (This is what the formula really means: Outside the Church, no salvation.) This is no doubt why St. Paul and the early Christians were optimists and we are pessimists. Am I going to get my salvation, we wonder, trembling. Christ is risen, the Church saved, proclaimed Paul triumphantly.

[8]Read Ezek. 33:1-9; 3:17-21; the doctrine on this responsibility is expressed in very measured terms. Hotheaded militants have

perhaps to relearn from this that a certain apostolic anguish is at times no great help.

[9]This bit of theology takes the moral aspect another step forward but also leads to the problem of vengeance. Until then, when a just man suffered (illness or persecution, all seen as punishment from God), it was possible to tell him, "It's your grandfather's fault, he sinned; or the fault of a sinful king; or the people's fault." But nowadays, what if I am given my personal desserts, or if I am innocent and still I suffer? Job had the same problem; it will be mentioned again later.

[10]The resurrection of the body is not intended here, for it will not be clear to Israel for another 400 years yet.

[11]This passage from Ezekiel should be kept in mind when reading, shortly, the first account of the creation.

[12]"See, your sins are forgiven you." This gives the sacrament of penance its aspect of confession; we confess and proclaim that the love of God is a wonderful thing.

[13]Go back to Ezek. 36. The Christians are responsible, or "signs" of God. By their means or ours can he sanctify his name. Our Father's demand is no platonic affair. We demand of God that he take away our stony hearts (and it hurts) in order to appear as holy in us and through us.

[14]Known by the letter "P," referring to the so-called Priestly Code, or "Book of the Priests."

[15]"Mystery that makes a man tremble and draws him" (think of the open sky high in the mountains); the fine definition is from R. Otto, On the Sacred.

[16]Praying depends not only on ourselves. What God wants of us is the disposition to prayer; whether he grants us the grace to feel his presence thereafter is neither here nor there. Joy of learning that black Carmelites will be allowed to dance before the holy sacrament. "Believe me," added the missionary who brought me news of his bishop's decision, "there will be no slow tangos."

[17]It is only when one begins to understand something of the role of the contemplative (and "useless") orders, that one may perhaps begin to understand who God is.

[18]See in particular the texts on the consecration of the firstborn

(Exod. 34:19; 22:28; 13:1-2; 13:13-16) and concerning the Levites ("consecrated" ones whom God accepts in place of the newborn) (Num. 3:12-13, 40-50; ch. 8).

[19]Perhaps they were helped by the fine poem, Ps. 8. Inspired by the second account of the creation, the author sees the world like a rainbow tapestry by Jean Lurcat with man, the point upon which creation converges, becoming a hymn to God through him.

Ps. 104, on the contrary, though relationship with an Egyptian hymn to the sun god (composed by Amenhotep IV?) is evident, might draw inspiration from its own setting.

[20]Genesis, history and geology. It is left to you to attempt a history of the life of Jesus, without forgetting his height and the color of his eyes, using the one source of the Gospels as the Church has us read them in the liturgy, and in that order. There is no harm in the pursuit. You can even prove this account goes against history and biology, since you will find Jesus preaching before we have been told of his birth, etc.

I have too much respect for you to believe you could possibly fall into an error of the kind with regard to the first chapters of Genesis. "What was it that the author wanted to say?" always remains the key to interpretation of the Bible.

[21]Quoted from Teilhard de Chardin, *The Divine Milieu,* trans. Bernard Wall (New York: Harper & Row, 1960) pp. 36-37.

Many other biblical accounts are from the Priestly writers. See the references in your Bibles. Mention may be made, in short, of genealogy of the patriarchs from Adam to Noah (Gen. 5); the priests' taste for blood relationships, which is recognizable, ensuring at least juridically and often by a fiction purity of blood., the extraordinary longevity (longer elsewhere, see the sacred texts of Sumeria), which is evidently of theological and not biological character (the number of years of Enoch, for example, 365, the same as for one solar year, or of Lamech—777: 7 is the perfect number—indicate to a sufficient extent the author's intention was precise; we do not know what it is, except there certainly was one!)

Account of the flood (Gen. 6-8, amalgam of J and P). See the note in your Bibles. It is instructive to compare this account with the well-known Babylonian versions. Utilizing the same themes, the sacred author has been able to give his account a spiritual depth which is utterly dissimilar. In the same context, note the liturgical character of the passage: the word for the ark by-the-by only occurs in one other instance, for the basket which saved Moses from the Nile; the ark has the measurements of Solomon's temple and the dates indicated correspond with liturgical dates.

[22]After Father Pautrel.

[23]Title of G. Auzou's commentary on Exodus.

[24]For the time being, we will omit the four poems (inserted in these chapters) called the Songs of the Suffering Servant of Yahweh; see pp. 114-116.

[25]Look again at the Gospel, ref. from Isa. 40:3. When John the Baptist says, "Make a way through the wilderness," he is stating that this is the exodus, the definitive liberation by Christ (that is, the Messiah). The definitive exodus is celebrated each year by the Church on Easter, and is made actual each day in the Mass. Exodus—each Christian is charged with the mission to make actual for his place and time. Exodus, last, when John in Revelation describes for us the end of the way in God's Kingdom.

[26]To sing of God's love for us, Second Isaiah found moving accents and formulas that St. Thérèse of Lisieux never tired of repeating. See, for example, Isa. 49:15-16; 54:7-8, and notes.

[27]The administration was well run, a memorandum of this edict giving the main points was kept in the archives. Twenty years later Darius had a search made for it; cf. Ezra 6.

[28]Good accounts are given in the histories of Herodotus and Xenophon.

[29]In the book of Zechariah, the message of two prophets needs distinguishing. The first (Zech. 1-9) is an apocalypse (see later in connection with Daniel, p. 174), whose often obscure message parallels that of Haggai: the temple must be rebuilt.

Deutero-Zechariah (chs. 9-14) announces for the future the final deliverance of the people. Four texts closely parallel the four songs of the Suffering Servant of Isaiah and show us this deliverance obtained by a mysterious shepherd rejected by his own people. Those who pierce him, when he is put to death, turn repentant, and this opens the way to forgiveness for them. Jesus applied himself, point by point, to fulfilling this prophecy:

Palm Sunday, he will enter Jerusalem on an ass, as the humble Messiah announced in Zech. 9:9-10.

He will be the Good Shepherd of Zech. 11, who gives his life for his sheep. When you read the story of the Passion according to St. Matthew, pay no heed to whether Judas actually got the thirty pieces of silver and threw them into the temple treasury; remember, rather, that it was the price at which the the people valued God (Zech. 11:12-13). For Matthew, the notation was primarily a theological one, in betraying Jesus, they betrayed God.

John will cite Zech. 12-13: in piercing Jesus, they pierced God. But from his side flows on us the fount of living water (John 7:38; 19:34-37).

To end, the final chapter (Zech. 14:6-21) will nurture the people's hopes in Christ's time, too, awaiting the coming of God's Kingdom.

[30]The prophet Obadiah tried to do the same. In this, the shortest message of the Old Testament, may be read—going beyond the cries of hatred against Edom—the certainty of the glorious Kingdom promised to Israel, and therefore God's, to cast down the mighty from their seat and exalt the humble (4, 19-21).

[31]

61 "The spirit of the Lord is upon me"	
60 The new Jerusalem, God's promised bride	62
59:15-20 Vengeance: the divine avenger	63:1-6
59:1-14 Two psalms: confession of sins	63:7-64:11
56:9-58 Reproaches. Promises to faithful. "Mother" Zion	65:1-66:17
56:1-8 Conditions of entry to people of God	66:18-24

[32]Among the dozen reconstructions, exercise care in selecting. I choose Father Pavlowsky's book, without regarding it as definitive.

[33]Some authorities attribute the two books of Chronicles to him. At all events (in the earliest stage, the two books of Chronicles, Ezra, and Nehemiah were all one work), this book tells us about history from Adam to Ezra. Earlier, it was seen how God causes history, "prophetic" history, to be written. The author of Chronicles goes over the same history to read in depth the unfolding of God's same plan. Since the time when the books of Samuel and Kings were written, prophets—Ezekiel in particular—have refined the religious meaning. The author tries to make us dis-

cover—beyond the anecdotal stream of events—the destiny of this people, both a messianic kingdom in line with the promises made to David and a religious community ruled by priests and living continually in the presence of God, the Holy One.

[34]Turn back to the definition of parable, p. 129. I say nothing of the jokes in poor taste about Jonah and the whale. The first thing to do is to see what the author wanted to convey.

If you read *The Little Prince* as though it were a historical narrative, you are missing the message of the book by Saint-Exupéry. Seen like this, the big fish (there is no whale anyway!) has great importance: he gives us evidence that, if need arose, God would be ready to overturn the natural order rather than leave his Word unfulfilled.

V

TIME OF WISDOM

"Spare the rod and spoil the
child: that is wisdom"
Sirach

"All the people shook with fear at the
peals of thunder and the lightning
flashes, and sound of the trumpet and
the smoking mountain; and they kept
their distance. 'Speak to us yourself'
they said to Moses 'and we will listen;
but do not let God speak to us, or we
shall die.'" Exod. 20:18-19

Word of God—human wisdom

There is a world of difference between these two
quotations: one is straight from heaven, the Word of God
Almighty, the Word that creates out of Genesis, the redeeming Word that frees us from sin. And the prophet,
Wordbearer of God, feels the crushing weight of the
reality imposed on him even when he can bear no more:

I used to say, I will not think about him,
I will not speak his name any more;
Then there seemed to be a fire burning in my heart,
imprisoned in my bones. Jer. 20:9

It is therefore known from the outset that this Word
is transcendent.

But it took fifteen centuries of education for God to
teach us the Word was to draw near to us, "the Word
made flesh." This name of "verbum" (Word) given to
Christ will remind us unceasingly that he is from God and
is God.

Wisdom is quite the reverse, being out of human knowledge, the experience of former ages transmitted (with what active methods!) from father to son. It is the fruit of our activity. Human reflection, often down-to-earth, a phrase expressing popular wisdom or a philosophic thought as produced at the same period by the wise men of Egypt or of Babylon.

It is therefore known from the outset that this wisdom is a human thing and our very own.

But it took fifteen centuries of education for God to teach us that the little girl Wisdom who, we thought, was our daughter, is God's daughter too; she plays in his presence and shares his throne, the handmaiden by whom he made the world and who one day came down to "live among us." To describe Christ as featured in the wisdom of the Old Testament will serve as a constant reminder that he is very much one of us and with us, a child of our race, man.

Twofold way for God to reveal himself to us, to make us aware how transcendent he is, the "All-other," and how immanent, the "All-near"; a double way with the coordinates at time's crossroads bound together in the person of man-God.

Double way profoundly marking those whom God involves therein. The global vision of Jesus Christ perceived so differently by John and Paul is an indication:

● Paul: Christ appearing to him on the road to Damascus to make him pass swiftly, with a turnabout of his whole being, from the most bitter opposition to the most passionate love.

● John, at the end of a two-year period very close to the Lord, gradually discerns that his friend is God!

Among the prophets we find the thunderclap of Paul.

The Word of God, a "consuming fire," a "keen-edged sword," is manifest by them in efficacy as an act of God, doing, making history, taking man over entirely, "ravishing" him. Life under the force of the Word is a struggle, a battle, a race: the "love of Christ driving us on."

With the sages, as with John, the process is one of slow discovery, no dramatic development; the wisdom one has always known is quite other than had been believed. Slow and amazed discovery that we have always lived in the company of the wisdom of God: "she was created with the faithful in their mothers' womb" (Sir. 1:14). Then all the old saws, the "proverbs," however humble and prosaic, become meaningful as the first attempts at utterance on the part of divine wisdom. Born in us, wisdom tries through us to grow and make us grow, taking us to the point of God; in the same way, the Child in the manger, having received his body of us, will take us to the bosom of the Trinity.

Proverbs

If you have not already done so, begin by opening this book and dipping into it at random (omit chapters 1 to 9, we shall be returning to them later).

The first contact you find disconcerting? A set of sayings, some wryly humorous, most rather weird, revealing a middle-class mentality, misogynous (e.g., "A golden ring in the snout of a pig / is a lovely woman who lacks discretion"). What is the interest of these proverbs?

Yet they are inspired and therefore God's message. How read them?

To begin with, a definition. The "mashal" (proverb) is a "case or situation of real life which excites attention or causes reflection" (A. Robert). On condition of giving the word "fact" a wide meaning (fact, act, word, reflection expressing a turn of mind or common attitude), this can be expressed in more modern language: the "mashal" is a "fact of life," a "fact of reviewing life."

If we take this definition seriously, it will transform our reading. There will be no more uncertainty as to whether or not spiritual improvement can be achieved.

If you consider this book a summing up of moral tenets, you will be disappointed, and justly so. In the same way, you could not get at the moral attitude of the average church member by up-to-date statistical data on the make-up of the membership of the church group Proverbs, to my mind, seeks to give us some awareness of our mentality, forcing us to think like Christians. Does not the least fact, if regarded in the light of God, make a man review his whole life?

The proverbs represent the oldest phase of the wisdom of Israel. But God continues the education of his people and, quickly matured by experience and having shed all human expectations, Israel reaches the age where the big questions have to be faced about the people's existence and the meaning of their lives, the why and wherefore of suffering and evil and the meaning of human love.[1]

JOB

Why Is There Suffering?
>Shadow of well-being
>and fate terrifying:
>God faithless and lawless
>masterless God who is Godless
>in accounting to none
>for those living and gone.
>>>>Marie Noël

If you never felt bad seeing a young girl disfigured, if you never felt ashamed of your health in front of a sick child, if you never found yourself almost demanding"Why?" like a blasphemy in spite of yourself, then do not open this book. For the time being, Job has nothing for you.

But if—your faith taking a beating because it leaves you nonplussed—you felt you shared something in common with the man who said, "If God existed, then evil would not exist"; and if to see a mother with her dead child could make you pray, with Marie Noël, like this:

> To you the right All-powerful one
> my flesh and blood from me to rend
> To you the right, O Mightiest One,
> to death our sons condemn,
> For you are God and you are good
> And you are . . . No, cries my blood!

then take this book, for that is where it begins.

It begins like a play by Anouilh. (Or better, like a classical tragedy. With this book, we find ourselves in the fifth century; **The Persians** by Aeschylus was written post-480 B.C.). "As the curtain goes up, all the characters are on stage. They are talking, knitting, playing cards. The prologue steps aside and comes down front" (Jean Anouilh, **Antigone**).

The prologue, here we are. The characters are going to enact for you the story of a man, Everyman, you and me, who suffers and does not know why. He was a rich man, happy with his wife and children. Now he has lost all: wealth, health, children, honor. He is sitting on a dung-heap. Man in revolt. His wife comes to remonstrate with him, and then come three friends who give him their good advice, and then even a fourth. But they are puppets. Only Job is real. For him, suffering is not some problem for discussion but a constraining reality that makes one shout.

In this drama, we say that the only character who is real is Job—and that means every one of us; each of us, when suffering, comes to bite into the skin, his own or others; here we are, you, me . . .

It is time for the play to begin. Act 1 opens.[2]

First, here is the program.

The Prologue (chs. 1-2) and Epilogue (41:7-42) are prose and only serve to frame the drama. The meaning of the book lies elsewhere.

ACT I

Scene 1: Job and the three old men   (chs. 3-27)
      Chorus of Miners   (ch. 28)
Scene 2: Job's lament   (chs. 29-31)

I N T E R VA L   (chs. 31, 40)

ACT II

Scene 1: Young Elihu and Job   (32:1-36:21)
      Chorus of Levites   (36:21-37)
Scene 2: God's speeches   (38-41:6)

Notes for further reading:

Job 3. "Why give light to a man of grief . . . to those who long for a death that never comes?"

Why are children born without arms? Why give life to someone dying of cancer?

Job 4-5. Or, "religion is the opium of the people."

Eliphaz, like his fellows, is a pious man. More, he knows his catechism: God is just and so he punishes the sinner. No comment necessary. By misfortune he is a man of the age and for him punishment can only be material, illness for example. So he thinks on these lines according to the theology current then (and still current today), reasoning like this: If you are ill, then God is punishing you and so you must be blameworthy. How fortunate you are to suffer here below, you will have less to suffer in purgatory (5:17).

Job 6-7. Job feels himself on the verge of blasphemy. "May it please God to crush me quickly, this thought would give me comfort . . . that I had not denied the Holy One's decrees."

Job 9-10. Job starts accusing; God not only permits evil, he wants this particular suffering to occur, and since suffering, to Job's mind, is punishment for sinning, then God has declared that he, Job, is a sinner who is innocent, in order to play cat-and-mouse with him!

Job 13. God is wise, Zophar has been saying. Job has something to answer. Stop it, you charlatans! Theology has no answer to suffering. Speaking of heaven to assuage the suffering is insulting God.

This insensate demand begins to glimmer through Job's talking: if only God, God transcendent who crushes, would diminish to my size then I could have it out with him and call him to account before the tribunal.

Job 19. Because he suffers, Job alone is real and he keeps on bringing the argument back to true ground while the old sages keep leading him away; it is God himself who is the oppressor, assailing him on all sides. "Two things are atrocious, Job says: God is either too near or too far away" (Neher). God has him by the collar and is strangling him, and when Job cries to him for help, then God is far away and there is no answer!

With a bound, like a child throwing himself forward with a cry of "Mama" straight into his mother's arms—and she corrects him, Job throws himself into the arms of God (19:23-26). But without unclasping his arms, God says nothing.

Job 21; 23-24. Job finds himself alone again and his accusations harden; he dares claim now that his case is not unique. Lines like those in chapter 24 have perhaps no parallel outside the terrible pages of **The Brothers Karamazov** on the suffering of children, or the death of the child in **The Plague.**

Job 28. As in ancient tragedy, the chorus comes on stage to express the spectators' feelings. Job's whole drama is that he suffers and does not know for what; it is God who oppresses him and God who is "wise." How acquire, in order to understand, the secret of wisdom? The chorus of "men of the lamp" prepares us for the climax: the miners know the earth's secrets, but the secret of wisdom, where is that to be found?

Wisdom is the fear of God, that is to say: the infinitely respectful and trusting love shown toward God!

Job 29-31. Job brings the Act 1 to a close by examining his conscience. How moving it is to see him considering his duties to his neighbor.

Job 32-36. The speeches of Elihu are a curtain-raiser, one has suggested with some justice. But there they are and thus inspired. For a man of the theater, vital. The first act ended with a climax; now the public's attention has to be newly aroused. God has been charged to present himself, increasingly, and he must be allowed the time to get there.

Job 36-37. It is the role of the chorus of Levites to introduce him. One can imagine Honegger writing the score, "crescendo continuo," fortissimo for the brass, and then suddenly, in complete silence, God's voice is heard.

Job 38-41. The stage is empty except for Job prostrate. God is talking from the wings. But because the stage cannot stay empty for long, God lets himself be seen, as Job has been insistently asking, by parading before the man's astonished eyes the marvels of creation.

Job 42:1-6. The real conclusion of the drama. Job prostrates himself in adoration.

The Epilogue, as in the best stories, rounds everything off; "they were married and had lots of children"; but the religious meaning of the book lies elsewhere: in the speeches of Job and those of God.

The meaning of the book of Job: it is the mystery of suffering in the heart of a believer, and the reply given him by God.

Mystery of suffering

On reading what Job has to say, bit by bit one word looms hauntingly, "Why?" "Why am I suffering? Why am I who am innocent the one to be struck? Why do the wicked prosper? Why illness? Why death?" and so on.

All the world's suffering, incomprehensible suffering, senseless, meaningless suffering, it is all contained here.

Mystery of suffering in a believer's heart

What makes this dialogue dramatic is that it is addressed to someone. "Why have you, my God, forsaken me? Why have you, who made me in love, struck at me? Why do you not answer me?"

The drama of Job is that he believes in God. But

that is the point where everything gets mixed up. This God is good and just. But he strikes unjustly. This God is all-powerful and yet he says nothing.

What overwhelms Job is not his friends' sarcastic remarks but the silence of God. In the great emptiness opening up outside him and within him, Job understands better and better that only God can save him, and God says nothing.

When at last God does appear, what is expected is that he will explain himself or at least comfort Job by promising him rewards.

God's only answer while showing Job the natural order is to say, "What right have you to ask me questions?"

So Job has "seen" God. He casts himself down in adoration.

What then has been gained by reading these forty-two chapters?

In respect of notions, nothing! Or little, namely, that traditional theology, at best, is sometimes no more than opiate in effect.

God has not inspired this book to teach us something, since there is nothing to learn in it.

But to make us discover a religious attitude.

"This attitude of soul is the humility of the small child who recognizes he does not know the last word about everything, especially his own existence, and accepts to the very last of the consequences his creature condition; from then on, he is not surprised to find himself embarked on an adventure about which only his Maker knows what happens along the way and in the end. To suffer in peace is for the man who has stopped wanting to understand his life in his inmost being, who takes refuge toward and against everything in the thought that this life, sometimes so inhumanly snapped off, remains yet the work of an all-powerful and good God" (A. Feuillet).

But did there have to be forty-two chapters to get that across? The only persons who could say that are those who think it easy, because they have not tried to "become little children again."

It was necessary for someone at length to utter our cries under suffering, for us to know that our "blasphemies" can be more agreeable to God than pious words. "You have not spoken well of me like my servant Job," God will say at the close to the three theologians who spent their time defending him!

After Job, it will remain for us to learn that that in itself can be a prayer. "My God, why have you forsaken me?" This is the cry of Christ on the Cross, the beloved Son of his Father, and it is the cry of Job, our suffering, and the blasphemy of the man-in-the-street turned into prayer. Of course, even then suffering is going to remain as incomprehensible to us as ever; we shall, however, know, as Job perceived but far better than he, that this cry can become, together with that of Jesus, a prayer of redemption for our brethren and ourselves.

QOHELETH (OR ECCLESIASTES)

A Christian Kafka?

"Everything that exists is born without reason, goes on for weakness and dies by mischance."

Kafka, **Nausea**

Crit, c-ze

Job suffered in his skin and bones: "Why suffering?" Qoheleth expresses the metaphysical anguish: "Why life?"

A strange book. An existentialist diary in a style deliberately drab and tiresome. Looking for a meaning, a goal, Qoheleth rejects all those that are offered him, whether theology at its most religious or Epicureanism:

> . . . wind, all chasing of the wind and deceiving, only one thing counts and that is good food.

Qoheleth pours the corrosive irony of his disillusioned skepticism on all our fine hopes and reasons for living, even on our notion of God. The drama: he rejects all our solutions as to life's meaning because he is too bighearted for them. But he does not know what to put there instead.

Austere but salutary medicine. "One of the rare writings of which it may be said that he who begins it as a child ends it as an adult" (Pautrel).

The Easter sun rises high only on the far side of the dark night of Kafka.

With Qoheleth let us enter his dark night.

The **meaning of history** and the Great Day? Nonsense (Eccles. 1:1-11).

The prophets believed history was ever new; they saw it progressing by an inexorable march onward to the Great Day when God would establish his Kingdom.

"Don't make me laugh," Qoheleth says, "with all your hollow words. History? Always the same. All vanity," etc.

(Would this be tantamount to present-day existentialism's answer to the overly human hope of Marxism?)

Well-being? Chasing the wind (Eccles. 1:12-2:26).

"Let's consider an outside case," Qoheleth says. "I put myself in Solomon's shoes, the great king, the wise man who had tasted all pleasures and well-being. Wisdom is no more than stupidity and folly."

Life? Death puts man in the ground, the same as a dog (Eccles. 3). Our life is meaningless and if not, then the meaning cannot be known, which amounts to the same thing. The end of life is death.

"Who knows if the spirit of man mounts upward or if the spirit of the beast goes down to earth?"

Social life? It is the crushing of man in society (Eccles. 4:1-12). "Open your eyes, society is the tears of the small people and the power of the gallows. There is nothing for it but to welcome death and while waiting, go humbly about the daily round helping one another, for 'one thread may break but two hold fast.'" (Read 4:7-8; the anonymous society was not born yesterday.)

Political action? An absurdity (Eccles. 4:13-16).
> Better a lad beggarly yet wise
> than a king old and yet foolish.

Religion? "God is in heaven; you, on earth" (Eccles. 5:1-6). Apologia for atheism? At the least, condemning our easy assurances. Be in no hurry so say, "Lord, Lord" or to go to Mass, because afterward you must practice your religion.

Money makes for well-being? "Those who love money never have enough."
> Man toils but to eat,
> yet his belly is never filled
> Eccles. 6:7

Harsh medicine it is. "All the aims you give life,"

Qoheleth says, "are nothing but wind. They are unworthy of man. Your heart is far too big for them."

But what about God?

"Yes, I know very well," says Qoheleth. "There is God and there is what is written in books about him. But all that? Nothing but wind."

God rewards and punishes on merits?

"Yes, I know, well-being comes to those who fear God and misfortune to those who do not. I know it well, but it is all wind because there are just men who get what the wicked deserve and wicked men who get what the upright deserve. It is all wind."

"But would it not be better than to be dead?"

"Ah no," Qoheleth says. "The living one is far superior to the dead one, because what he knows at the least is that he will die. The man who is dead knows nothing."

Love. Qoheleth deals with it in "melancholy, tact and respect" (Pautrel). "Spend your life with the woman you love, through all the fleeting days of the life that God has given you under the sun; for this is the lot assigned to you in life and in the efforts you exert under the sun" (Eccles. 9:9).

Chance. "Fault nothing, what ought to have happened does not." Yet Qoheleth is an optimist and concludes, "Of two things, you do not know which will happen. So, roll up your shirt-sleeves and do both."

Hoard old age. "Do good so that you may have long life." "We have been told this—wishful thinking—until we are dizzy," Qoheleth says. "Old age, it means decaying."

Yet he falls for it. In a little picture that is admirably poetic (yes, Qoheleth can be a great poet, but it tires him), he describes the old man at his threshold, for us to see. He gets so carried away by his emotion that his real thinking shines through at last. "Before the dust returns to the earth as it once came from it and the breath to God who gave it," etc. (12:7). He quickly recovers, not to let his disciple see him so emotionally involved, "But it is all wind," "Vanity of vanities," etc.

That is his last word. Life is absurd. God exists but he is in heaven, indifferent to man, who has to get by on his own in a world where God seems absent.

TOBIAS

God Works in the Everyday of Our Everyday Lives

The book of Tobit takes up where Qoheleth left off.

The narrative centers on a double case of the just being made to suffer. Tobit, the father of Tobias, is a model of faithfulness to God and the victim of a stupid mischance, and Sarah is the victim of an evil spirit.

Both are mocked by their households. Tobit's wife says to him, "What about your own good works? Everyone knows what return you have had for them"; Sarah's servant-girl says, "Yes, you kill your bridegrooms."

Both say a prayer and ask for death, life not being worth the pain of living any longer.

Life apparently is absurd. But from the end of chapter 3, the reader is let into the secret: God is present in the life of Tobias and Sarah as in the lives of each one of us. But he is hidden there. It is up to each individual to divine God's presence.

The whole book is a response to Qoheleth. The narrative breathes an atmosphere of peace, of domestic tenderness, of simple joy. Misfortunes are not suppressed, certainly, but the absurdity of life is. The world has meaning; it is intelligible, because God works there, but has to be sought out. Then one perceives God has a plan for each of our lives.

Indeed, God had a very precise plan in view for Tobias and for Sarah; by this, the book becomes the text on Christian marriage.

Marriage is a vocation, a call of God

Genesis taught us this. In the beginning, God made Eve especially for Adam. But afterward, what about their children? How did they manage? God teaches us in this book that for him the creation of each home is an adventure, as new as the creation of the world.

Tobias and Sarah have not met; several thousand kilometers lie between them. But God has prepared them for each other and so they cannot be happy except together: all other attempts fail. God wants to have them meet and so does not hesitate to make the world turn over. One has the impression that the exile (the national catastrophe that completely changed the people's history) had no other aim but to bring Tobias and Sarah together. God does not hesitate, either, to intervene directly in history. The angel Raphael ("God-heals") comes down with a very precise mission: "his job was to cure Tobit and give Sarah as bride to Tobias" (3:17).

Marriage is the meeting of two beings whom God has prepared for each other, whom he has "called" from time everlasting to meet each other (6:18).

Thus brought about, marriage finds again its original destiny:

Marriage: human love leading to God's love

The whole tale is told in a climate of "God's blessing." One has the impression that in this climate of grace, marriage finds again its clear purpose as a sign, since it is in and by marriage that husband and wife find God; their mutual love leads them directly to God.

Read the admirable prayer of Tobias and Sarah before they are united (8:4-8), a "prayer to put one right in the line of vocation."

It begins with a freely given blessing.

Then Tobias recalls the plan of God, what God meant in creating marriage: the achievement of two beings by each other, mutual completeness which becomes fecund. Then he pursues this line; he is not taking Sarah for "pleasure" (a pejorative term, it is not in order to satisfy himself egoistically by her means), but he does it "in truth," meaning "within God's plan" where "all God's ways are grace and truth" (3:2).

Vocation of the man, which is to be responsible in the Lord for his wife (10:12; 7:11; 6:18).

Vocation of the woman, who by giving herself to her husband is to transmit life (6:18).

What a marvel is marriage! In this climate of grace, that of the world's dawning for Adam and Eve, that of the new creation by Christ, man and woman in and by their human love find themselves within God's love. In a climate of ideal grace, free from sin, the love-song of the affianced man for his promised bride will be a love-song of God.

This is the whole meaning of the Song of Songs.

THE SONG OF SONGS

"Ah, how fair the world is and how happy I am."

Violaine

"One may read in the second account of creation (Gen. 2) of that which refers to man and wife. There Israel, moved like other peoples by the feeling a man and wife have for each other, has written from the bottom of her heart" (Audet).

God had made Adam and in all the headlong rush of his young splendor, Adam was off to conquer the world. But gradually he became aware that something was amiss; he was alone, he was short of "achievement," and his enthusiasm waned. The whole wide world held no interest for him; he went to lie down.

When he awoke, there appeared before his eyes, taken by God from his heart (the modern equivalent for the word "rib") Eve. Then there burst from his lips, full of wonder, the first song of conjugal love, "Ah, that was it, heart of my heart!"

The Bible transmits to us Adam's cry of joy but says nothing as to what Eve felt. She was going to keep it for a whole book!

The song is first a song of human love, like those the bridegroom-to-be and his promised bride sing on the wedding eve. It is the orchestration of the song that Adam sang, and repeats two of its themes:

• marveling contemplation of each other (contemplation which leads to desire of union)[3];

● association of nature, of all creation in this joy.[4]

It is very probable that the Song of Songs for a long while had only this meaning.

But it is certain that later on the Jews made an allegory of it, celebrating the love of God for his promised bride, namely, his People (Do you remember Hosea, Jeremiah, Ezekiel, etc.?). They thus opened a source of interpretation; into it, all the great mystics have zealously dipped; it slakes our thirst to be loved (and to know it) personally by God.

Perhaps the literal meaning-in-depth of the song is to be sought in another direction.

The love-song of Adam (Gen. 2) was interpreted, in effect, some centuries later by the priest-theologian who wrote (Gen. 1:27):

> God created man[5] in the image of himself,
> in the image of God he created him,
> male and female he created them.

The image of God is not only, it seems, the man or woman but, first, Man, meaning the human couple. The image of God, that is, the gift between people. This brings us back to the essential and unique gift between the three persons in the Trinity. "In the bosom of the intimate life of God, One in three Persons, the Father and Son live eternally, a mystery of union, and of their loving union the Holy Spirit proceeds. One may in truth say that the mystery of the life of God is contained in these two words: union and fecundity. That is where the analogy bases itself, by grace of which marriage is in the image of the life of God" (Father Lucien Marie).

One remains speechless at such perspectives: the

marveling of young people in love thus becomes a human and very poor but real echo of the eternal marveling of God contemplating himself in the Trinity. Is that not one of the best stepping stones for the discovery of God-love for all the many homes where there is true love, but no knowledge of God's existence? For as long as we are on the earth, it is by the mediation of human love that we understand something of the eternally young love that is of the essence of God's love, and also that we are preparing ourselves to "Enter into the joy of [our] God."[6]

[1] Only Father Pautrel will recognize my debt to him, very great in this context.

[2] I know the scholars discuss the authenticity of this or that extract—see the introduction in your Bibles—and endeavor to reconstruct the original work. But let us say once again, in the present book we decided not to deal in detail with the history of the composition of the books (though not ignoring this question), in order to have time to read the books as transmitted to us by the Church.

The work God inspired is in the end the text such as we have it. If, therefore, reading it like classical drama helps us to get at the religious meaning (as Father Pautrel suggests, none too seriously), we are being faithful to God's Word.

[3] The part describing physical attributes may be found to be considerable. But love often begins there and the body is God's handiwork. One must not be put off, either, by the "sexual component of this love." "Shame is a universally human feeling but the social taboos that ensue are variable, sometimes opposite, from one environment to another. The Song describes the almost naked body of the two who are betrothed but shows them prevented by public opinion from embracing in public. If a modern equivalent had to be sought, it would emerge in the Scandinavian countries" (Dubarle).

[4] A word of explanation to guide further reading. Some expressions may seem childish to us (no more so than the mawkish

words that lovers use nowadays to express their tenderness). One must not—counter to the procedure in the Jerusalem Bible notes—seek to transpose each image but only bathe in this climate of love. Follow the advice of St. Bernard: "In this epithalamium, weigh less the words than the feelings."

[5]"Man" here meaning "man and woman."

[6]Praising marriage, with the Bible, in this way, I do not intend to decry consecrated virginity. It is, on the contrary, the point of achievement, and will be referred to later.

VI.

GOD'S PROMISED BRIDE,

HER FAITHFULNESS TESTED.

HELLENISM

1   **Mirage of Humanism only Human. Alexander and the Ptolemies**

His family album on his knees, God is dreaming . . .

Everything considered, things have not gone too badly. In spite of various crises—but he is good at turning them to advantage, even with sin—the education of his first-born, his people Israel, is going well.

He looks back over the ground that has been covered since the obscure beginnings, those marvelous early days when the people loved him perfectly because he was represented in a man, the father of this people, Abraham, his friend. Then, he—God—brought this people to birth over the Red Sea waters, by his Word on Sinai, by means of his servant Moses. Next comes David, the young ardor of a people working to their full capacity to build an earthly kingdom, a draft form of the true Kingdom: "It is I who will build you a house." Alas, temptation was too strong and the people thought the draft form of the Kingdom was all there was to it: the shadow ended in hiding the reality! Then God's hand was needed to restore order; he recognized that he had to act a bit roughly, but the forty-nine or fifty years of exile, so well prepared for by Jeremiah, were fruitful. His people, this promised bride of his whom he loved even when unfaithful, had come back to him solely because he—God—had continued to love them.

And now this people have settled down once more in Palestine, endowed with precise law thanks to Ezra (attention, pharisaism!). His unfaithful promised bride has become the virgin he loved again, a small remnant of poor men abandoned in his arms. And this bride-to-be has grown up (witness the real problems she is asking herself now, about the meaning of life and suffering and love). So God is going to make her fruitful, "Zion" will give birth to the new people, their Messiah.

Before that, God has to perfect their education:

• Education in faith. Religious reflection must be made deeper in them, by meditating on the mystery of Wisdom, to welcome and recognize Wisdom when she comes one Christmas night to "put up her tent among us."

• Education in hope. By means of suffering persecution, the people must await more eagerly the Day of God and learn to await it from God's hands only.

• Education in love. These closing stages of preparation are going to be one of the longest. It is faithfulness in love that God wants to test. Faithfulness which must withstand the usury of time, God's silence (no more prophets to come, and no one knows for "how long," as the psalmist cries), and especially the temptation, a terrible one, of human wisdom, of human effectiveness.

His family album on his knees, God is dreaming . . . About the plan of love he has in his heart; but of course he is not going to express it just like that to his people.

God does not speak directly—not in those times any more than in our lifetimes; he speaks through events.

On the plane of events, the history of Israel is only that of a little people at the mercy of the great powers.

The Victory of Samothrace . . . floating in the unreal spotlights at the top of a staircase at the Louvre. This winged Nike—what is her date, 200 or 250 B.C.?—remains the best symbol of the man she led for thirteen years and over 18,000 kilometers from one victory to another, from Macedonia to the Indus: Alexander.

333 B.C.: the victory of Issus opens the Middle East to him. Palestine submits. 332: he founds Alexandria in Egypt. 331: he is at Babylon, Susa, Persepolis. 325: the Indus. And in 323 he dies of malaria at Babylon, this young king, thirty-three years old, who has built many Alexandrias in an empire 5,000 kilometers wide, spread Greek culture,[1] and more especially, perhaps, created the means to unity that a common language comprises. This name of "koine" ("common" language) that the Greek tongue is to bear henceforward is evidence enough of the character of universality acknowledged as belonging to it. It will be the language of the New Testament and the translation of the Old Testament.

The battle of Ipsus in 301 will bring to a close the twenty-year war among the "Diadochoi" (the generals who "inherited" the empire): the Ptolemies became masters of Egypt, the Seleucids of Syria and Asia Minor. Between the two: Palestine. For a century (301 to 198), the Ptolemies constituted the law.

Domination of the Ptolemies

A one-hundred-year peace.

These descendants of Alexander's companion Ptolemaeus (most of them bear this name) are good fellows. Convinced of the value of Greek civilization, they will strive to spread it, never doing so by use of force. In the peace of these years without history, Judaism deepened. Novelty: this unique religious nucleus is going to have two poles, from now on, one is the traditional one at Jerusalem; the other is newer, at Alexandria.

Alexandrian Judaism

There had always been Jews in Egypt.[2] Now they are going to form a particularly active group in the new cultural capital of Alexandria. Authentic Jews, they read with fervor the law of Moses or, rather, they would like to except that they no longer know Hebrew! So they set about translating the law into the Greek common language. Perhaps ca. 250 B.C. the Pentateuch was translated, and the other books followed, with differing literary fortunes. This accounts for the origin of the Septuagint[3] version. Event of the first importance; "the Greek Bible is going to become the fast-moving world-traveling vehicle to convey the revelation made to Israel" (Auzou).

These Jews of Alexandria will be spiritually openminded enough to admit to their canon of inspired books, a certain number written directly in Greek.[4]

Palestinian Judaism

Drama in Jerusalem. Is parliament going to give way? The members of the religious party in parliament have resigned. Press campaign throughout the country and in Jewish circles throughout the world. Very tense atmosphere in the city. Debate in the chamber. And the origin of the conflict? The building project for a public bath in the Holy City.

Is it 300 B.C.? No, it is not. It is the year of our Lord 1957, but the old place has not changed and the analogy is illuminating.

Let us put ourselves in the position of a young Jew of the strict sect living in the Mea-Shearim quarter of Jerusalem. For him, there is one and only one absolute value: God. God and his Word. And God the Holy One has chosen him, a poor Jew, to live in his presence in love and serve him with respectful fear. He also knows that this God is not dealt with man to man but "as a people." He is aware, when he prays and when he is serving him, of entering a tradition, of being carried to him on a whole stream of history. But a tradition is not something unreal, it means concrete custom and practice in matters of diet and dress (kosher food and those terrible long black coats), prescriptions and prohibitions.

Then he bumps into a band of boys and girls from the kibbutz nearby. Religious drama in his heart. He envies the harmony of the young bodies, their brightly colored shorts showing off their tan. He envies the joy of living in their laughter. He envies their pool, their work, and their ideal. But he feels this envy as a temptation because all these young people are Marxists. Their god is the future of their country; their bible the glorious myth of the past. This modern state they have created and which they symbolize, he finds abhorrent with his whole believing heart as the sin of Israel, claiming to build them a kingdom when the true and only Kingdom must be by God's hand when his Messiah shall come.

It is not a question of judging but of understanding this suffering and his greatness, also of understanding that this suffering must necessarily be our own as we are Christians.

It is the greatness of these pious Jews, at a time when they think that their faith in God and their desire to live on earth are incompatible, to come down on the side of God.

It is the suffering and the temptation of every Christian in the face of the current tide of Marxist socialism, feeling himself powerless because he has not the right to be effective by borrowing the other man's arms. During this time, the Church is falling back on all sides, sociologically and geographically. The suffering of the Christian worker because, as of now, socialism and Christianity seem incompatible, and in the eyes of a great many people, being socialist means giving up Christianity.

If you replace Marxism by Hellenism, then you have the picture (just about) for the third century B.C.

But then, has the history of Israel nothing in the way of teaching for us? God's message then, is it not a message for our time as well?

ECCLESIASTICUS (SIRACH)

Message for Our Time

"My grandfather, Jesus ben Sirach, having devoted himself more and more to reading the Bible was brought to the point of himself writing down some of the things that have a bearing on education in wisdom, in order that men might make all the more progress in living according to the law. For you to be able to profit thereby also, I have translated it into Greek—with pains and diligence." Thus, in the year 132 B.C. this model grandson wrote the opening for his grandfather's work.

This Jesus was therefore writing ca. 190-200 B.C. A wise old man, a bit middle-class, he felt the attraction exercised by Hellenism over his contemporaries. Drawn by this humanism, many people were finding the law with its old-fashioned rites rather hard going and were taking the risk of welcoming the new fashion like a liberation. So he decided the time had come to take pen in hand. His book is the "reaction of an intelligent man, determined to defend traditional values and the sacred inheritance of God's people" (Auzou).

In the face of the temptation of purely human wisdom— Hellenism it was then, as Marxism nowadays—his message is a peaceful affirmation and a clear one that the faith is sufficient, that true wisdom is given by God. Before this temptation, the answer was faithful trust in the Lord, to abandon oneself in full confidence like a child in the arms of God.

One must not, therefore, expect him to have practical advice for social or political action; that was not the end he had in mind, but the spiritual climate in which one has to dwell to face the times, accepted as a fact and over which he helps us to cast a Christian look.

The second part of the work (chs. 42-50) is the better structured.

It shows us, first, God's glory in nature (chs. 42-43).

He wrote especially for his readers the Eulogy of the Ancestors (chs. 44-50). This holy history according to Ben Sirach "is a perfect model of the spiritual reading of the Scriptures. He chooses freely from the lives of the fathers the facts that would be meaningful to the people of his time and come across, if one can put it like that, on a topical note" (T. Maertens). Collecting the most religiously significant features of these Old Testament saints, he to some extent sketches in advance a portrait of Jesus.[5]

The first part, the longer (chs. 1-42), is in the best wisdom style. Look not for logical pattern but for a series of aphorisms developed in differing ways and on differing subjects. It will be enough to go through the first six chapters and discover the fundamental themes. The rest of the book only elaborates them.

Sir. 1:1-20: wisdom, in God and man.

This wisdom, the aim of all philosophy and living, that Hellenism claims to be able to deliver, is possessed by only one being: God. He made wisdom to give her to those who love him.

"Who love him," meaning "who fear him." The Hymn to the Fear of God is comparable only to St. Paul's Hymn to Charity (see 1 Cor. 13). It begins abruptly, introduced by the words, "to love," since "love" and "fear of God" are one and the same feeling (with an overtone of worship in the second).

"Wisdom: she was created with the faithful in their mothers' womb" (1:14). Between wisdom and the man who fears God there is thus a companionship out of faithfulness: it (the word is "faith") goes to the man who cherishes wisdom and God (in French, too, the same root-word for faith, faithfulness, confidence, and betrothal).

Sir. 1:22-26: how to get wisdom.

There is a pre-condition, 1:27-30.

What God wants at the outset in the man who wants wisdom, "faithfulness and sweetness." "Faithfulness" or faith, the devotion of the whole being; "sweetness" from the Hebrew "anaw," "poor," as one who abandons himself in the arms of God like a baby with his mother. When we come to the word "humble" (or, rather, "lowly," meaning "poor" but with an extra overtone of humility: "He has looked on the lowliness of his handmaiden," see the Magnificat), we shall have the three fundamental notes on which Ben Sirach builds his synthesis,; so fundamental there may on occasion be some risk of not hearing them— like the pedal in an organ-piece—the three fundamental notes of each and every Christian life offered God in love's symphony.

There is a second condition to be met, once one has started (Sir. 2):

> My son, if you aspire to serve the Lord,
> prepare yourself for an ordeal.
>
> Sir. 2:1

The seeking of wisdom (not static contemplation but a seeking out; many words seek to describe it, pursuit, a striving after, etc., and it is a pity that the Jerusalem Bible has rendered them by abstract terms); the search for wisdom is no easy path: God tries and tests the man who seeks it. This examination demands "lowliness"; one has to be made very small to be carried to the arms of God (2:17; 3:17-29). This lowliness will help us to love the needy with a poor man's heart (3:30; 4:10). In this passage, "the idea of divine paternity, one of the peaks of Jewish thought, is expressed in admirable fashion: when man heeds the unfortunate like a father, then God will heed man like 'the father'" (Hadot).

The book of Sirach describes the way in which wisdom educates us (4:11-19), indicates what the "poor man" in whom wisdom puts her trust is like (4:20; 6:4); next after showing us that the touchstone for all true friendship is this very lowliness (6:5-17), the conclusion comes with the finding of wisdom (6:18-37), thus: "You have started out

. . . you have been tested and come through. . . . I have shown you the model of a poor man, . . . now you must know that until your hair is white you must go on seeking. Give your shoulder to her yoke and take up her burden (they are light), think well on this, . . . and the wisdom you desire will be granted you."

We come thus prepared to the crisis. A passage (4:20-31) admirably sums up the attitude of the believer (of the Christian), a paradoxical mixture of humility and security. Sirach is a realist; it is not a question of getting holy quite outside of time, life has to be faced as a fact (no lamentation for our period) and one has to know how to meet it (4:20); to be able to tell the difference between one kind of shame and another, the one leads to sin (shame to seem Christian) and the other is a glory (the Christian cannot avoid, one day or another, being despised, as his Master was; see, for instance, Heb. 12:1-4). No false humility, "When you know, speak out," etc.; but do not be ashamed of knowing yourself a sinner before God. Last, and this covers the whole Christian mystique in times of persecution, to know when to give way, to be despised but to fight on (no false defeatism) to the death when the truth is at issue: "The Lord God will fight for you."

This is exactly the message Israel needs in the year 200 B.C.

2 Test of Force. The Maccabees

Seleucid domination

It is 198 B.C. Syrian elephants overthrow an Egyptian army; the era of martyrs is about to begin.

At Paneion (the future Caesarea at the Jordan's source), the army of Antiochus III is fighting the Egyptian general,

Scopas. Palestine passes under Seleucid domination. Unlike the Ptolemies, the Seleucids tend to impose Hellenism by force. In fact, there are a few happy years still to go. Antiochus III is intelligent; he confirms the privileges of the Jews, who keep full liberty for the practice of their religion. But in 174 there succeeded to the throne of Antiochus, one who would engrave his coinage with the surname of Epiphanes (God "manifested") and which would be corrected to that of Epimanes (the "mad"): Antiochus IV.

In 170 he proclaims himself king of Egypt and profits from his passage through Jerusalem to swell his treasury in the best tradition of his family: he sacks the temple. In 168, he goes to Egypt again, where he comes up against a very unimportant Roman consul who asks him haughtily to go back where he belongs. Forced to temporize, Antiochus the madman lets loose in Palestine the Great Persecution. In 167: massacres in Jerusalem. "Abomination of Desolation": in the temple of the living God a statue of Jupiter Olympus is erected. The altar is destroyed, sacrifices abolished, circumcision and the reading of the law prohibited, and the Jews forced to sacrifice to the pagan gods. All this on pain of death. Read 1 Macc. 1; 2 Macc. 5-7.

That same year, the control commission turns up in a little village called Modin. The leading inhabitant is a priest, one Mattathias. An altar is erected and the order given to make sacrifice to the gods. A Jew comes forward. With a bound, Mattathias is on him and slaughters him there on the altar together with the king's commissioner. After that, there is nothing for him but to take to the hills, along with his five sons. It is the start of guerrilla activity. The fifth son is called Judas, soon to honor the family by the second name of "hammer," Judas Maccabaeus. Success in the hill country of Samaria. Judas defeats a colonel. A general is sent against him: Judas defeats the general. Two generals are sent against him: Judas kills one and puts the other to flight. The governor of Syria moves out, but as the king then dies, he negotiates with Judas and returns to Antioch. On December 15, 164 B.C., exactly three years after the abrogation of sacrifices in the temple, Judas purifies the holy place and restores the daily sacrificial rite. The festival of dedication commemorating the event will—in the time of Christ—be one of the most solemn events in the liturgical calendar.

With Judas, Israel regained her freedom of religion. When this is taken away from the people again, it will be A.D. 70 and will mark the end of the nation.

Maccabees, or Hasmoneans (167-40 B.C.)

Strange fate. Their history begins cloaked in the blood of martyrs and ends in the tatters of Herod.

Judas gained freedom of religion. His brother Jonathan (160-143) achieved political independence by some skillful maneuvering, turning now to Syria and now to Egypt. Meantime he bought, without the right to hold it, the office of high priest. Simon (143-134), second son of Mattathias, obtained a rescript which he was able to interpret as a recognition of autonomy: the year 142 became year 1 of the new independent state. John Hyrcanus, his son (134-104), remade the kingdom of Solomon. Period of political peace.

But the Pharisees, the most religious sector of the people, began to form open opposition to the Hasmoneans. It led to eight hundred of them being crucified under his windows by the son of John, Alexander Jannaeus (103-76) because they called on Demetrius of Syria for aid against the descendants of the martyrs! The reign of Jannaeus (he assumed the title of king) marked the high point of the dynasty. After the reign of his wife Alexandria (76-67), who looked to the Pharisees for support, severe decline set in.

When Pompey came to Syria in 63 B.C., a delegation from the holy nation came and begged him to set them free. Fratricidal wars, venality, assassination. But as in decay a plant may produce its finest flower, from this morass there emerged two bright young figures: Aristobulus, beloved of the masses for his gentle ways and drowned because of it on the orders of his black-hearted brother-in-law; and his sister Mariamne, with all the nobility and distinction of her race, their pride also. When the Bedouin of the Negeb, the self-made Herod, son of Antipater the Idumaean, married her in 37 B.C.,[6] three years had passed since he got from Rome the title: King of the Jews. The title only with permission to conquer his kingdom. And under this bloodthirsty madman's regime (he had one member of his family after another put to death, as well as others), being skillful politically, Palestine knew a comparatively peaceful spell.

Since it was during this period that Israel developed different groupings, political, social and religious, which were to stamp subsequent internal history, some account of these will now be given.[7]

Social classes

Their origin is evidently an ancient one, often obscure. It will suffice to name:

The **people of the land;** in the time of Christ this meant the unlettered, despised by the aristocracy, often ignorant of the law and its details.

The **scribes** are the experts in the law, and laymen in particular, who have dedicated their lives from childhood to the study of the Scriptures. Their upright living and knowledge of the law make them directors of the conscience of the people who respect and love them in return. Most are Pharisees.

The same cannot be said of the **priests**, at least of the high clergy. The high priest (the choice from the time of the Hasmoneans gladly rested with the highest bidder), after his pontificate, sometimes very brief, kept the title. Thus there came into being a kind of upper caste called high priests, comprising family and friends. This priestly aristocracy as little religious as possible, of the Sadducee party, hated but feared by the people, must be distinguished from the 18,000 or so priests and Levites who were close to the people and performed their job with piety.

Religious sects

If you open the Gospel, it will be found that of the three main sects there was one constantly under attack by Christ and another which he despised. The third is not referred to.

The **Pharisees** are the holy ones of the Old Testament. Descendants of the Hasidim[8] who fought against John Hyrcanus, their piety obliged them to increase the distance between themselves and those Jews who were ready to make terms with Hellenism (this may be a possible explanation of their name "separatists"). "In general, the Pharisee is above all a highly religious man, concerned for the holiness of God and trying to make plain that the relationships of man with such a Lord, if possible and marvelous, are of no easy access. He is a disciple of Ezekiel" (Auzou).

Meticulous interpreters of the law, they held that interpretations collected by tradition were equally valid along with the law.

Their sin, to have confused end and means. They believed that rigorous practice of the thousand-and-one precepts was enough for loving God; they got to the point of deeming their salvation deserved on account of their efforts, no longer as a free gift from God. Jesus denounced their pride but was anxious to put them right "because of the esteem he had for them and the influence they wielded" (Auzou).

The rest were all **Sadducees.** Political opportunists, ready for any religious compromise so long as they held onto power, they wanted to keep strictly to the written law. They claimed to interpret it with great vigor: lax in all domains, they found themselves in the position of being unbending in penal matters. Materialists, they believed in neither angels nor the resurrection and did not admit the influence of grace upon man. It was the priests' party.

The **Essenes,** unknown in the Gospel but mentioned by Pliny the Elder, Josephus and Philo; they have come to the fore lately with the discovery of the Dead Sea Scrolls.[9] In the time of Jonathan, they parted company—like the Pharisees but more radically—with that impious priest and his followers, and organized a separate community under the guidance of their Teacher of Righteousness. In the wilderness[10] by the Dead Sea, they founded the monastery of Qumran where their communal exercises were conducted: the sacred feast, the council, and the copying of the Scriptures and sectarian documents (the celebrated Scrolls). The remainder of the time they dwelled in the nearby caves. They were celibate (a kind of lower order for married men existed in Damascus and no doubt elsewhere). They held their goods in common and were assiduous in their study of the Scriptures, in prayer (the psalms of their founder are remarkable for piety), the feast of the bread and new wine and in regard to the teaching of their masters.[11]

3 Literature of the Maccabean Period

Sensing the crisis threatening to engulf the faith of Israel, Jesus Ben Sirach tried to detain the spiritual climate necessary to deal with the mirage of Hellenism, to deal eventually with persecution, "to fight for the truth to the death."

Persecution had come. Double reaction: taking to the hills and martyrdom. The Jews went down fighting, some with arms in their hands and others abandoning themselves to God's mercy.

Sacred literature remaining to us from this period reflects these different options. It may be classified in three categories:

1. Call to arms: war literature, part of the running fight of the Maccabees.

2. Call to God: mystic or "escape" literature; the sword, even that of the Maccabees, seemed ridiculous. So much was God's intervention expected that it was thought no human help was necessary. These are the apocalypses.

3. Call to brotherhood: once the struggle is over and traditional values safeguarded, then the policy is one

of the hand of friendship and assimilation of the valid content of Hellenism.

1 AND 2 MACCABEES
Call to arms

First Maccabees, "one of the best history-books of antiquity" (Auzou), belongs at the same time within the frame of reference of the "earlier prophets": if it describes in excellent fashion the triumphs of the Maccabees, it is first and foremost for the sake of showing us God at work, in freeing his people by saving them from the evil to which their sins had led them.

Second Maccabees is more closely related to some of the Lives of the Saints. The history of heroic figures is a pretext for moral or doctrinal teaching. It thus affords precious evidence of the faith of Israel at this period. Here one finds attested for the first time belief in the resurrection of the dead (2 Macc. 7:9; 14:49) and the efficacy of prayer for the dead (2 Macc. 12:38-46). Here also the interceding role of the saints in heaven is explained to us (2 Macc. 15:12-16).

THE APOCALYPSES
Call to God

The apocalyptic genre is one of the most baffling for modern readers, it appears. Yet for the space of several centuries, this kind of literature was very popular. The Bible preserves two masterpieces in this genre: Daniel and Revelation.

The Greek Bible grouped Daniel with the prophets. That is not false, for continuity exists between the two literary genres. When the point of despair has been reached in human terms, the prophetic genre readily turns apocalyptic.[12]

The prophet's mission: to enable his contemporaries to live fully in the present, by showing them the end purpose of history, namely, the building of the Kingdom of God as it will come to pass on the great day. However far he tries to see ahead, the prophet always comes up against the luminous veil barrier: it marks the end of his foreseeing and at the same time hides from him what will be.

While work goes on to build the Kingdom, this is the message to maintain hope. But when loyalty to the faith only means offering one's neck to the executioner, when the nation seems destined to be engulfed entirely because of the faith itself, then hope must be fed on more than promises; there is a need to see right into the future, to draw back the veil ("re-veal" in Latin, "apo-caluptein" in Greek) and contemplate what lies on the other side of world's end.

The author does not necessarily have to have had real visions. His message of hope does not belong on that level. In fact he has no "revelation" to impart as to the future (certainly not the date of Hitler's death or the end of the world!). The author is a prophet, primarily, who can discern in past history God's usual working method; from this, the prophet can teach something about the future. It is like a high-jumper who goes back to get a good run at the point of take-off, being impelled forward in the same direction. The author of an apocalypse adopts the fiction (pseudonymous procedure) of being a personage out of the past (e.g., Daniel, who lived four hundred years before the author of the book of Daniel). This enables him to run through history (which he knows well but may not "predict"); then in his own period, forward he goes, still in the same direction: God who has saved his people in the past will do so in time to come.

The only thing is, that the seeing is not enough. Words have to be found to express it. Paul was "lifted up to the third heaven" and what he heard there was "ineffable" (2 Cor. 12:4). The visionary lacks words to tell what he has seen; the one who makes an attempt, risks being diminished; by means of images (the more out-of-the-way the better),[13] he transmits to us not what he has learned, which is impossible, but what he has felt. It is like a painter making an attempt with daubs of color that "do not mean anything." It may well be that more than one apocalypse is inspired to transmit to us not truths about the "other side" but feelings when face to face with the same. The feeling that predominates is hope. All human interventions, even the most saintly, then seem derisive; the only thing to do is sit and wait for God to perform a sudden act of intervention in history.[14]

DANIEL

This book comprises two quite distinct parts.

The first (chs. 1-6) is a review and an interpretation of the Scriptures for purposes of edification.

The year is 165 B.C. when the persecution of Antiochus is at its height. Yes, I know the author begins, "In the time of Nebuchadnezzar king of Babylon." But put yourself in his position; it was no time for writing, "God will make Antiochus IV a brute beast," etc. So we agree, Antiochus is to be replaced by Nebuchadnezzar (dead 400 years), then all will be peace and quiet. About the year 165 B.C. our author wanted to encourage the unfortunate Jews in their time of trial. To achieve this, he hid the key to his message under the cloak of history. The reader finds one within the other.

The people were crushed by the power of Antiochus. He felt at a loss, however, before the colossal might of succeeding empires, Babylon, the Medes and Persians, the Greeks with their two offshoots in the Ptolemies and Seleucids. (The composition of each strand is in itself instructive; Antiochus was common clay compared with the gold of Nebuchadnezzar!). The poor sword of the Maccabees seemed ridiculous; their only succor was an act of God. And then a "rock crashed down the mountainside untouched by any human hand" and broke the statue into bits. Hiatus in human history; God is going to intervene in history at this point without the help of any human hand.

The three young men in the fiery furnace: the pious Jews, Pharisees and Essenes who read this—since they too had "disobeyed the king's command and given themselves up rather than serve other gods" (Dan. 3)—knew the message was meant for them. "Fear not, God will send an angel out of heaven to go with you in the fiery furnace and keep you from harm."

Even if you are put to death, God is still capable of bringing you alive out of the tomb. This is the teaching of chapter 6. For having refused to adore the king, Daniel is put to death, which is so necessary a consequence of his going down into the lions' den that the king has a stone put in position (funerary) and duly sealed before going into mourning. "If Daniel comes out alive, the miracle will have the value of a veritable resurrection of the dead." What happens? Daniel comes through the lions' den the same as the young men in the furnace:

unscathed, because he is the incarnation of the whole Jewish people, under assault by the forces of evil but protected from harm by the angel of Yahweh" (Steinmann).

The second part of the book (chs. 7-14) comprises the apocalypse strictly speaking. Some account will be given of the most important vision only, that of the Son of man (Dan. 7).

By using suggestive images, the author gives us a picture of contemporary history as it appeared in the sight of God:

Dan. 7:1-8, interpreted in 7:15-28; here are the four great empires, they are beasts and come from the sea, traditional haunt of the infernal powers.

Dan. 7:9-12, God (an Ancient, to indicate his eternity) sits in judgment.

Dan. 7:13-14, 27, to meet him there come the Jewish people, in the semblance of a man (thus, far superior to the beasts of empire) but a celestial man: he is not therefore the fruit of human endeavor (or the Maccabean blade) but of God's grace. The Lord is going to give sovereignty to the people now under persecution, and all the others will serve them.

The comfort of this parable, in faith, is already apparent. But the human author in the writing could not suspect all the riches God had included. We are going to know one day that the "people of saints" announced for the end of time are here already, once Jesus has said, "I am the Son of man"; and in process, since the Son of man is present in each of our brethren (Matt. 25:36 ff.); and that it will be finally set up when at the end of time, "you will see the Son of man coming with the clouds of heaven" (Mark 14:62).

The books of the Maccabees. War literature. By sustaining the fight of the heroes of Judaism, it will contribute its own part to the saving of Israel as a people. The danger, that of leading the people in the direction of the building of a kingdom purely of this earth (like the quasi-atheist kingdom of the Hasmoneans and Herod, where God served the lust for human power).

Apocalyptic literature. Mystic, "escape" literature. These "poor men" have got hold of the idea that God can save, that it only means awaiting him, all human intervention apart, to receive salvation. A call to God in confidence and resignation. The danger, that of wanting to be so holy, one forgets to be human (people, satirized by Péguy, with pure hands because they have no hands). Insofar as followed, this stream of thought risks leading to the disappearance of the people as a human reality. Its value, that of a reminder to the people that there is a kingdom primarily of the spirit, celestial. "My kingdom is not of this world," Jesus will tell Pilate. And John in the book of Revelation will see Jerusalem, the symbol of the Kingdom we are building by all our human endeavor, come down from heaven because this is the Kingdom given us by God.[15]

In the conflict between God and the world—on the cosmic level (Hellenist humanism) or the historical—these two streams tend to one of the two extremes.[16] Beyond (and after, speaking historically) brutal opposition, it will be the merit of some wise men to try and strike the balance.

Wisdom of Solomon
Call to brotherhood

"Somewhere a point of view ought to be found whence Christ and the world

would appear so situated, the one relative to the other, that I could not
possess the one without clasping the
other, commune with the one without
fusing with the other, being absolutely
Christian because so desperately human."

Teilhard de Chardin

When Greek culture and Jewish faith met (and the
ground was no doubt in Alexandria), this book—the last-
written of the Old Testament—was composed directly in
Greek ca. 50 B.C. "The author is addressing himself to his
fellows in religion who might be led astray by the prestige
of profane thinking and to strangers drawn by the spiritual
nobility of the monotheist faith" (A. M. Dubarle).[17]

Of its two parts, the former is the more speculative
and the latter a reflection starting from history.

PART 1: "There is no true wisdom without true religion."

The author proves it in two stages: by opposing wise
men and wicked men (chs. 1-5); by showing that only God
gives wisdom (chs. 6-9).

Wisd. 1-5: the destinies of good and bad men will show
the wisdom of the former and the folly of the latter.
"Wisdom comes like a spirit from God, dwelling more
deeply in man than his own self" (A. Lefèvre). Letting this
spirit work in us, that means life; refusing to do so, means
death (Wisd. 1). Outwardly, on earth we all "exist," but
in fact this existence is life or death (or, which comes
to the same thing, existence unto death). At the point of
our carnal death what each of us is in depth will be
visibly manifested.

The wicked (Wisd. 2) are in fact friends of death. For-getting that "God made man incorruptible by making him the image of his own nature," they think it is all over at the grave and that the only rule for living is having a good time, mocking the upright whose austere life seems absurd. (The evangelists will show us this impiety at work in the Jews—and in us all as sinners—mocking the Upright One on the Cross. See the marginal notes of references in your Bibles.)

The upright, on the other hand, at the judgment will appear what they already are in a hidden manner: the only ones who are alive. Striking contrast between the fate in store for them and the wicked:

Wisd. 3:1-12: the apparent absurdity of the life of the good and their reward (they will live close to God in love) in the face of the punishment of the other kind.

Wisd. 3:13-4:6: What is a fruitful life? The barrenness of the upright will produce lasting fruits (working up to the virginity consecrated to God and its marvelous fecun-dity).

Wisd. 4:7-19: the agonizing problem expressed by Job and others: the well-being of the wicked and suffering of the good ("What is the good of washing my hands in innocence?" Ps. 73) is here given one of its definitive answers. Untimely death is not the sign of condemnation on God's part but, on the contrary, a sign that the "dead man" (lit., "de-functus," the one who has stopped function-ing) has achieved the task God entrusted to him on earth, attaining "perfect spiritual stature."

Wisd. 5: the Godless at the judgment will admit the emptiness of their existence; "scarcely born, we have ceased to be," whereas "the virtuous live for ever because the Most High takes care of them."

Wisd. 6-9: the high point of this book, dealing with the "personality" of wisdom, its origin, nature, and how it is to be obtained.

Solomon (in Jewish tradition he remains the type of the wise man; attributing to him a work composed 1,000 years later is not to give a false label but denotes the literary genre which has been selected pure and simple), Solomon the wise tells us how he got hold of wisdom; it was by prayer. He shows us how to pray to God for wisdom (9:1-18) and recounts the immense benefits he has gained thereby; his one joy is to make us share them. Above all, he gives a description of this wisdom which the New Testament authors will one day be applying to Christ, "eternal wisdom of the living God" (7:21-30).

PART 2: Wisdom at work in the past history of Israel (hence in our history at the present day).

Wisd. 10-11:3: wisdom in the life of the Fathers (symbol of what it does in our own lives). Seven examples are given, ranging from Adam to Moses. It was wisdom who delivered Adam and directed Noah. She chose Abraham and "fortified him against pity for his child." She saved Lot and showed Jacob the Kingdom of God. She went down to the dungeon with Joseph. She entered the soul of Moses and by him she led the people along a marvelous road.

Wisd. 11:4-19:22 (leaving out the long parenthesis of 11:15-15:19 which opposes God's forbearance as man's friend—admirable prayer 11:21ff.—and the stupidity of idolatry): God's love for his people appears in history from the time they left Egypt. The same seven elements are at once Egypt's downfall and the Jews' salvation:

- water from the rock and the blood-red water of the Nile (11:4-14);

- the animals, harmful to the one and nourishment for the other (16:1-4);

- the locusts and the bronze serpent (16:5-14). What cured was not the bronze serpent but God, the "universal savior" "by his all-healing Word";

- the hail and the manna. "Creation does its utmost to punish the wicked and is the universal nursemaid of the good: by giving them angels' bread, creation teaches them it is your word that preserves those who believe in you" (such texts have passed unaltered into our liturgy to stand for Christ's work in the church);

- when the wicked are in darkness, the saints of God are in light. But they must "transmit the imperishable light of the law to the world" (17:1-18:4);

- the death of the firstborn of Egypt, the people's ransom, "God's firstborn." The Church utilizes 18:14 as the opening song of the midnight Mass, the child in the manger is thought of by the Church as God's all-powerful Word but—here the quotation must end!—he comes not to bring death but brings upon himself the death we deserved;

- the Red Sea water that kills and the water of baptism (of which the Red Sea is the sacrament) which gives life (ch. 19). It is by redeeming nature that God has determined to save us: foundation of the theology of the sacraments (see the prayer, "Deus qui humanae substantiae," of the Offertory in the Latin Mass).

Among the many riches in this book, certain teachings are singled out for mention:

One must "commune with God through the world."

"Reconciliation is possible between the cosmic love of the world and the celestial love of God" (Teilhard de Chardin).

God does not mean to take the believer right out of the world; on the contrary, he is launched to conquest by having his place in this universe and the role he must play revealed to him. "Israelite wisdom remains what it was from the very beginning, an invitation not to detach oneself from the world but to make use of the world for the glory of God" (A. M. Dubarle).

The world is good. It is born of God's love (11:24-26). "Death was not God's doing; to be—for this he created all; the world's created things have health in them" (1:13-14).

Man is God's work too, but with a unique distinction: "God made him in the image of his own nature" (2:23; this image, which is finally wisdom herself—7:26—and thus Jesus Christ, Col. 1:15). Man is God's son (2:13, 16, 18; 5:5; 12:7-21; 26:10, 26; 18:4-13; 19:6). He therefore has special relations with God, he will remain close to him in love (3:9-10; 7:7, 16).

Man in the cosmos. Nature has been corrupted by the devil's envy (2:24) but was newly fashioned by God "to keep his children from all harm" (19:6), since the wisdom of God is the designer of the universe (7:21) and she is all purity, she penetrates everything, leading back to the loving kindness of God (7:24-27).

The cosmos is given to man, who can penetrate all; there are no more prohibitions ("To all who are pure themselves, everything is pure," Paul will tell Titus; Tit. 1:15). Everything is given man so that he may give God all:

> in your wisdom you have fitted man
> to rule the creatures that have come from you,
> to govern the world in holiness and justice
> and in honesty of soul to wield authority
>   Wisd. 9:2-3

but the prayer continues,

> grant me wisdom, consort of your throne.
>   Wisd. 9:4

All this will not be possible unless wisdom comes and dwells with men. Here we get down to the main teaching of this book. But as what is told us about the origin and nature of this wisdom is the climax of a train of thought, it is necessary to review briefly the great biblical texts dedicated to the same.

The concept of wisdom in the Bible

PROVERBS

The Proverbs represent the most ancient stage of stored knowledge in Israel.

In the Hellenist period, a wise man crowned this gathering of proverbs by the magnificent canopy of chapters 1-9. He is the first witness to the progressive personification of wisdom. She begins to speak out for herself: preaching like a prophet (1:20-33); by her, God created the earth (3:19); she cares for the one who loves her (4:6). To keep from harm, not to fight against temptation but take refuge in the love of wisdom (ch. 7). She calls to all human beings (8:1-21) and invites them to her table; when Dame Folly hands out a lethal dose, Dame

Wisdom offers us the true repast of communion; Jesus takes up the terms in John 6.

Replace the word "wisdom" by the name of Jesus and you will be astonished at the facility with which you will be able to pray with these texts, at the living portrait, and the true one, which you will have of Christ as wisdom incarnate.

This is valid especially of the most famous passage, Prov. 8:22-31, Song of the Infant Wisdom (Gelin). "Before she made progress among human beings, this lady of experience as old as the world was a little girl who lived for the love of God only."

"Yahweh created me . . . before the oldest of his works" (Prov. 8:22); literally, Yahweh gave me being—rather as a woman brings a child into the world—not "at the beginning" but as the beginning of his plans (his ways), as the prelude to his works.

Then creation is described for us. It is not said that wisdom created the world, but as this feminine figure—the only one individualized—who, holding God in Michelangelo's Sistine fresco looks at man fascinated, she does not leave the creator's side. "Her presence is that of a witness, with the charm—and secret influence— of a child" (Gelin). For it no doubt by "infant," little girl, that the word given in your Bibles as "master craftsman" must be translated (8:30).[18]

But that was "in time," in God's time, meaning, before the creation: firstborn of God for joy, the little girl wisdom is also going to come down among men to make the young cosmos vibrate with her joy.

This is expressed in another poem honoring wisdom:

BARUCH (3:9-4:4)[19]

"So causing wisdom to appear on earth
and move among men."

Bar. 3:38

The new element in this reflection lies in the identification made between this wisdom and the law. We thus begin to see how this daughter of God has come to be present among us. God has sent her—and she obeys with the same joy as the stars; at the call of God they joyously respond: I am here!—and this was the start of wisdom's arriving on the scene (from the Word of God by the law) all through the Old Testament ("She has come to her own," cf. John 1:11) until her definitive coming, when "After having spoken by the prophets, God has spoken to us by his son" (Heb. 1:1).

SIRACH (ch. 24)

Praise of wisdom.

One more step forward is taken. Wisdom is no longer identified only with the creative Word of God and the law, but with the holy presence of God in his people ("shekinah" of the Jews contemporary with Christ): "pitch your tent in Jacob" (Sir. 24:8), the same term John will use for the Incarnation. "He pitched his tent among us," meaning, he lived among us (John 1:14).

WISDOM OF SOLOMON

All these themes are summarized in this book to give us, in advance, the most explicit revelation of the very being of the incarnate Word. Here Paul will find the Word which is no doubt the binding element of his Christology; it will explain in elemental ideas what he understood in a flash about Christ on the road to Da-

mascus, he is the "image" of God (Wisd. 7:26). This becomes the point of departure for his thinking in the letter
to the Hebrews, that magnificent meditation on Christ's
priestly person. John was inspired by the same source in
his "Hymn to the Word coming into the world" (John
1:1-18) and throughout his work.

It is here, most important of all, that wisdom must
be replaced by the name of Jesus. May you then "fall in
love with his beauty" (Wisd. 8:2), "the friend of men,"
and "make him your companion in life." He will then
make you and all those into whom he comes in the course
of the ages," the friends of God (Wisd. 7:27), we whom
God "has predestined to become true images of his son"
(Rom. 8:30).[20]

[1]This culture established itself everywhere in the most per-
ceptible forms: gymnasiums, arena games, art, and theater—to be
remembered when we find the Jews refusing to countenance
swimming-pools.

[2]On Elephantine Island, facing Aswan village, there had been
a Jewish military colony from the seventh century B.C. It also
had a temple. The discovery of a cache of Aramaic papyri dating
from ca. 400 B.C. has greatly enriched our knowledge of the
history of Ezra and Nehemiah.

[3]According to tradition, the translation was made simultan-
eously by seventy interpreters, working separately, with one and
the same result. Thus the name Septuagint, "the Seventy."

[4]A double scriptural canon begins to emerge: the Jerusalem
one contains only the books written in Hebrew or Aramaic; the
Alexandrian one admits, in addition, works known only in Greek
translation or composed directly in Greek. Christians reading
the Septuagint version of the Old Testament will accept this
canon (last vestige of the canon, the title "deutero-canonical"
given to these books in our Catholic Bibles. Protestant Bibles
no longer print these books).

[5]Do you sometimes think of surrounding yourselves with these

grand Old Testament saints? Their rites have remained very much alive in Eastern liturgy and have not disappeared from the Latin liturgy, which has Masses proper to a certain number of them.

[6]He had her strangled, finally, in the year 29; then mad with grief, he ran through the palace shouting for her, whose body he apparently had preserved in honey.

[7]Experts will tend to close their eyes, regarding these as oversimplified general statements, overlooking my attempt to condense the subtle maze which the outlook of these people represents, with much remaining still to be investigated.

[8]The word "Hasidim" comes from the root "Hesed," love, tenderness toward God and other men (refer back to Hosea). Also called Hasids.

[9]The literature is vast; the best work is still the little book by an (one is tempted to say "the") expert on these mss.: J. T. Milik, *Dix ans de decouvertes dans le desert de Juda* (Cerf, 1957); Eng. trans.: *Ten Years of Discovery in the Wilderness of Judea* (Naperville, Ill.: Allenson, 1959). The same author, in collaboration with J. Starky, produced the excellent issue, No. 4 (July, 1957) of the periodical, *Bible et Terre Sainte.* (I have taken the views of Milik here, without discussion.)

[10]The word "wilderness" means something precise to a contemporary of Christ—as for us the name "Grande Chartreuse," for instance, evokes a monastery under a mountain bluff. John the Baptist in his youth went into "the wilderness."

[11]To describe the Essenes, I have intentionally used the words of St. Luke in Acts describing the primitive Christian community. Comparisons are possible between this community and that of the covenant, as it was called (which is the Greek word we translate as New "Testament"). John the Baptist spent his childhood within their sphere of influence (and John the Evangelist was first his disciple); the two communities have certain elements in common, and at least to outward appearances some rites, for example, the feasts and baptism. Can one go further and see—as some authorities do—convert Essenes among the Hellenists of Acts 6 or the recipients of the Letter to the Hebrews? In this context, reference may be made to the booklet (despite its rather hasty conclusions) by J. Daniélou, *Les Manuscrits de la Mer Morte*

et les origines du Christianisme ("The Dead Sea Scrolls and the Origins of Christianity"; Orante, 1957).

Do these manuscripts shed light on a hitherto insoluble problem, namely the chronology of the Passion? You may be aware that the Gospel of John and the Synoptic Gospels cannot be harmonized. Annie Jaubert has shown the Essenes followed a different liturgical calendar from the official temple one. Her argument, though there are tremendous obstacles encountered, would reconcile everything: Jesus, crucified on Good Friday, would have celebrated the Last Supper on the Tuesday evening. John, using the official calendar of the Pharisees, would not have reckoned the Last Supper as a paschal feast; the Synoptics, however, using the Essene calendar, would have done just that.

[12]The genre is now well-known through dozens of apocalypses that have come to light of late years, and more recently from the Qumran site.

[13]On images in the apocalyptic genre of writing: They are varied, touching on the celestial world: angels (in apocalypses they are part of the literary scene); animals, more often than not borrowed from Assyro-Babylonian sources; and in particular, numbers.

They are often incoherent or, rather, their coherence belongs in terms of idea not image, for they are all symbolical. This symbolism works for colors: white=victory, purity; red=the blood of martyrs or murder. For numbers, their meaning is not arithmetical but theological. 7=the perfect number; $3\frac{1}{2}$=half 7, meaning imperfection or suffering=time of testing or of persecution ($3\frac{1}{2}$ turns up in various guises but the value is constant: $3\frac{1}{2}$ or "1 time + 2 times + $\frac{1}{2}$ a time" or $3\frac{1}{2}$ years are of no longer duration than $3\frac{1}{2}$ days or 42 months or 1,260 days). 12 stands for Israel (ancient or modern). 4 is the cosmic number (because of the 4 directions ?). Numbers can be multiplied, e.g., 12 x 12 x 1,000 =144,000, the value of which remains in essence that of the number 12.

[14]This is the teaching to emerge from those two magnificent historical tales, the books of Judith and Esther. In situations which look desperate, God takes a hand (or, which comes to the same thing, he intervenes through the weakest human instrument available) to save his people, faithful or at least repentant.

[15]A word about the role which is complementary and sometimes conflicting (must it be so?) of the spiritual and the practical in a nation; also about the problem of Christian institutions: Does a free school, patronage, a well-ordered parish—and if so under what conditions—pave the way for the celestial Kingdom?

[16]Atheist systems of all times and all philosophies of non-involvement down the ages, from Hinduism to some forms of Christianity.

[17]Of all the Old Testament, perhaps the book closest to modern sensitivity. But be careful. The author may talk Greek fluently and use modern concepts (soul and immortality), but he remains a Jew and by the same words does not necessarily mean the same as we do. When he contrasts, for example, the "psyche" and the body, one would like to understand that man is made up of a soul and a body, as in Greek philosophy. But on this point in particular I think that our author is being very Jewish indeed, contrasting our "historical being" destined to corruption, with that "certain something" which outlives carnal death. Is that after Aristotle? One may be permitted to doubt it.

[18]A good opportunity to mention the richness of Hebrew and difficulty of translation! As in Arabic, the vowels are omitted (at least in the primitive text). The consonants 'MN (root found in the liturgical word, 'aMeN: it is solid, it is sure) can be vocalized here in a very slightly different manner: 'aMoN will be the present participle, 'aMuN the past participle. The participle standing for a noun, the choice, therefore, is between "the one who bears, founds," hence architect, master craftsman, and "the one who is borne," whence babe-in-arms, little child!

[19]No mention has so far been made of this book under the name of Baruch, Jeremiah's secretary. In fact, it comprises different extracts in literary genre and date. A letter of Jeremiah ends it, preceded by a discourse on consolation (to Jerusalem lamenting her fate, as in the Lamentations, a prophet produces a consolation analogous to that of the Second Isaiah). The book begins with an admirable psalm of penitence, Prayer of the Exiles. Meditation on sin is no morbid psychological self-musing; the meaning of sin presumes a feeling of absence, we are exiled far from God.

[20]Wisdom: the Christ or Mary?

This extraordinary figure of wisdom sharing the throne of God, creating, can clearly only stand for the Word Incarnate.

How can the Catholic Church apply these texts to the Virgin Mary (they serve as epistles on several feast-days)?

The suffering of our Protestant brethren before the verbal excesses of Catholics is, still more deeply, our own. These texts in their plenary meaning envisage and can only envisage the Christ. But this application made by tradition can perhaps help us be more exact: they envisage no doubt, in the first place, total Christ, meaning the Church, of whom Mary from now on is the figure.

VII.

THE PSALMS

> "We are born with this book in our hearts."
>
> André Chouraqui

1 **Soul of a People**

Israel: a people living in the presence of God[1]

> "King David then went in and seated himself before Yahweh."
>
> 2 Sam. 7:18

Nothing, to my mind, is as moving as these simple words. David, the king "drunk in the lord."[2] He danced until he was out of breath before the Ark of the Covenant. He will trust in God in suffering, consult him on all occasions, recognize himself unreservedly a sinner before God. But nothing touches this plain statement: David seated himself before Yahweh. The prophet Nathan had just delivered to him a message from God, "Your house will live for ever before God." His heart full heavy at this intimation, as one goes to see a friend and tell him what has happened, David goes into the tent where the Ark is kept and seats himself before God.

It is understandable that the Psalter should be attributed to him (and besides, there is no cause to deny all authorship in his regard). For his attitude provides the best definition of it.

The Psalter is what the people confide to God when, with full hearts, they come and seat themselves before him.

The heart full heavy with being so beloved, "You are great, Lord Yahweh," David murmurs, crouched before the Ark. "There is no one like you and there is no other God but you alone," the heart full heavy for having sinned. "You sinned against your brother by taking his wife from him and then by killing him," Nathan tells David; David answers, "I have sinned against you, my God"; "against you and you alone I have sinned" (Pss. 51; 6)[3]; the heart hamstrung because he no longer understands, "my God, why have you deserted me? I call, no answer. Yet you are the holy one, in you our fathers put their trust and you rescued them" (Ps. 22:1-3). "Do not betray your turtledove to the beast, do not forget your wretched people for good" (Ps. 74:19).

The Psalter is the confidence of the promised bride in the one she loves, the child babbling to his mother, the book of a people living in the presence of their God. Treating not of ideas, not even of feelings but of impressions, life simple and straightforward as lived by the open-hearted before their God.

> Yahweh you examine me and know me,
> you know if I am standing or sitting,
> you read my thoughts from far away, . . .
> you know every detail of my conduct. . . .
> It was you who created my inmost self
> and put me together in my mother's womb; . . .
>   Ps. 139, passim

The book of a people so true before God that each of us, in the course of the ages, finds himself expressed with all he senses.

Israel: a people where every individual talking to God says "us"

A preliminary remark or "apology for distractions during prayer."

"I had distractions during my prayers," one of the most frequently heard charges in the confessional. A highly ambiguous charge. You come to pray and begin by collecting yourself. Right; but what does it indicate, this phrase "collecting yourself"? I can hear your answer: casting out every thought but that of God. Which is all very well but isn't it forcing the sense a bit? If I say "collect" or "recollect" of a flower or a child, I won't mean casting them aside, surely? To talk of "recollecting oneself" means recognizing implicitly that I exist only in relation to others; that "I" is undoubtedly the being on his knees at the prayer-desk, but it is also the being relative to colleagues at work, family and friends, to all those for whom I am responsible, those to whom I am bound; and it is this "I" in so many places that I must remember to "recollect." Felicitous distractions God sends me just in time, to remind me that I present myself before him— not "alone" (that is not me), but that I must come to him as a "person," meaning, linked with all my fellow men.

It will be a matter of centuries for us to rediscover man's social dimension and collective responsibility. To Israel, it meant centuries to get a clear idea of individual responsibility! But it was never with them "individualist" responsibility. Each individual knew himself engaged in a dialogue called the covenant between God and his people. And God goes from you singular (the people) to you plural.

"For you are a people consecrated to Yahweh your God; it is you that Yahweh our God has chosen to be his own people out of all the peoples on the earth" ("you" singular).

"If Yahweh set his heart on you and chose you, it was

not because you outnumbered other peoples. It was for love of you and to keep the oath that he swore to your fathers [the covenant] that Yahweh brought you out with his mighty hand and redeemed you from the house of slavery" ("you" plural).

"Know then that Yahweh your God is God indeed, the faithful God who is true to his covenant and his love" ("you" singular again) (Deut. 7:6-11).

"Biblical man is never alone before God but always among brothers because he is the man of the covenant" (Gelin).

This is important in understanding the psalms. The "I" of some of them and the "we" of others refer to the same subject. But in the one instance the stress is on man's individual aspect and in the other instance on his social aspect.

This is important for praying with the psalms. There are in effect two ways of doing this, to be employed in turn.

"Individual prayer": I choose among them the psalm that best expresses my feelings at the time.

This way of praying is never to the exclusion of the other.

"Ecclesial prayer": that which the Church entrusts to the men and women members of religious orders (Breviary): I choose to have feelings expressed by the psalm I am praying with at this time. Is it possible and is it sincere? There are moments when all goes well, when I am problem-free and happy: can I sincerely say to God, "Lord everything is going wrong, raise me from the pit where I am sinking"? If, on the contrary, I am down-hearted at my sinning and that of others, if I am tempted and no longer want to love God, how can I truthfully say, "Lord, wonderful are your ways and all your works"? But when I as a priest open my Breviary, when as a layman I recite such a psalm in union with the Church by prayer, I am not offering God "my" prayer, expressing to him "my" feelings: I am the voice of mankind, the voice of all the people I have met, of all those also whom I have not met because they are far from God and yet I am responsible before him for them.

There is no better school for becoming a "universal brother" than praying with the psalms because in each of them (whatever my feelings at the moment), I am by turns the voice of those young lovers for whom everything is marvelous, of that mother weeping for her child, this chum who is fed up, that man who cried out to me, "If God existed, then all this would not," the voice of the rebel, the voice of the saint.

To pray well with the psalms, one must know better the Church whose voice I am, the world of sin and of grace. To pray with such-and-such a psalm, I must know before I begin whose voice I shall be in the praying, I "make ready the heart" in a different way when I go and call on friends according to whether they are in weal or woe; before reciting a psalm, it matters that I make ready the heart. Determining the literary genres is the function to help at this Juncture. We shall come back to it later.

Israel: a people on the move back to childhood

> "Once childhood is over, it takes a lot of suffering to recapture it, as after the night there comes a new dawn."
>
> **Dialogue of the Carmelites**

The Hebrew "anawa" is untranslatable. Yet it is the very word to describe man's fundamental attitude in the presence of God. It is usually rendered by "poverty" ("anawim," the poor). Anawa is what the poor man feels, marveling that someone can love him and that he can love, but with something of the childhood element about it too. "Childhood" is perhaps the best translation. Not the one that lies behind us (which is only "ignorance") but the one of Bernanos to which we go and which is a conquest. "Except you become as little children . . ." That of Job, passing from revolt to abandonment; that of David and of Jeremiah; that one day of Mary. That of the most "meek and mild" psalm in the Old Testament.

> Yahweh, my heart has no lofty ambitions,
>   my eyes do not look too high.
> I am not concerned with great affairs
>   or marvels beyond my scope.
> Enough for me to keep my soul tranquil and quiet
>   like a child in its mother's arms,
> as content as a child that has been weaned.
>   Ps. 131:1-2

Rather than going on about "poverty," just take a look at a living "poor man." For this purpose, it will suffice to·read the marvelous little group of psalms of various literary genres called the Psalter of Ascents (Pss. 120-134). With freshness and naïveté, the soul of a people is expressed in them, speaking to God and to whom everything speaks of God.

We have now outlined the three fundamental threads in the prayer of this people: the worship of someone who knows he is in the presence of his God; solidarity with his brethren before God; poverty or better, childhood, of the spirit.

The psalms reveal to us the religious soul of this people. Their imaginative qualities also.

2 Imagination of a People

The psalms are poetry—meaning—imaginative, free-wheeling.

The very opposite pole from those prayers which are magnificent, namely, the orisons in the Latin Mass. Heir of Roman legal concepts, whereby a word has a "value," but given inner meaning by the piety of St. Leo and others, Latin liturgical language has come up with certain untranslatable words for the treasures of God's love and of theology.

The Hebrew language is carnal, as Péguy used the adjective. Low in vocabulary, rudimentary in syntax, it offers only concrete words and images to express what its people sense. People born of God's love, they feel his heartbeat in the midst of nature; they are almost physically aware of his presence in the ear-straining silence of the blue nights of the East, they know his greatness in the dazed brilliance of the desert sun. The carnal world and the word to express it means for them an incantation of God. The world and the word, and the Word, is sacrament, losing nothing thereby of its carnal density.

Rationalists after Descartes, we were fully equipped to get along with other language. But Baudelaire and Claudel and Teilhard have made us relearn: to listen to the unanimous voice of creation caught in the magic of the word. The cinema has made us learn the value of symbol: an image is always something other than itself—a window on the infinite, man and God.

To pray well with the psalms, one must be a poet

or become one. Anyway, we must set aside our technical spirit, which turns everything into algebraic formulas, and everything is money, even time. One must give oneself up to the poetry of the book, let oneself be carried along by the "incantation of Hebrew rhythms." And then "slowly the soul of the psalmist becomes our soul, his fight our fight, his gentleness our gentleness, his anguish ours, that of all men who age after age have given their lives in this living flame. Slowly our soul becomes accustomed and takes nourishment from the eternal soul of the cantor of Israel, the brightness which overwhelms him strikes us, the light he asks for shines on us, it transfigures our shadows with ineffable joy. One voice lives in us and enraptures us: it takes from us our limits, makes us pass through the walls of our prisons, and weds us to the splendors suddenly more close to us than our very selves: one face leads us, one presence makes us fruitful, and on the road to true learning one song carries us through the night, in your light, Jerusalem" (A. Chouraqui).

3 Feelings of a People

In accord with the prayer of this people and with their imagination, it remains for us to make the heart ready with the feelings expressed in these prayers. In more mundane terms, we must study the main literary genres used in the Psalter.[4]

1. Hymns, or psalms of praise

The feature of a hymn is the joy, disinterested, springing from all authentic spiritual life, as in the Gloria of the Mass or the Preface. Not reasoning but marveling before God, because he is great, because he is beautiful, because he is God. The hymn is the very pure expression of religion because it places man foursquare before God: over and beyond our little problems, sufferings, death and sins . . . there is God, the joy of God. Man the creature can only sing his heart out with praise and admiration.[5]

The **literary structure** comprises three parts (e.g., Ps. 104):

(a) invitation to praise, "Bless Yahweh my soul," comprising an imperative, the name of the one to be praised, a call to those who must render praise;

(b) development expressing the motives of praise with mention of God's great deeds or his attributes; it may become a real account, here it is of the creation, or of the history of the people, the exodus especially;

(c) conclusion, repeating the invitation in a more personal way or, again, a blessing, a prayer, or an acclamation of the assembled people, "Allelu-Yah!" "Praise God" (Ps. 104:33-35). (Ref. this psalm, see also p. 131, n. 19).

The **doctrine:** this is joy in experience of God through two events, redemption and creation:

(a) the redemption, "God of history": first intuition Israel had thereof. Their God is the living God (the other gods are only "idols" and hollow "images") who chose Abraham and who saved his people "by the might of his hand" in the exodus.

Background to the hymn: liturgy, which "re-presents" that is, makes present anew, all the great deeds of God in the history of the people.

Celebration in advance of this God-Christ Jesus living in history to accomplish in his death-exaltation the definitive exodus, this paschal "passing" that the liturgy in its sacraments, marvels of God in our history, makes us live by "representing" them in our midst.

(b) the creation. If God can act in history, it is in that he is the master of the world. By reflection one will arrive at conceiving of God as the creator. This specific belief of Israel will not fear to express itself in terms of Canaanite or Babylonian mythology.

The full significance of creation will be revealed to us by the New Testament: it is by Christ and for him that the cosmos was made (Eph. 1:15-22). These psalms have thus quite naturally become Christian prayer.

Christian prayer: Eucharistic praise to God our Father, and a call: in his Son present by all the sacraments, for God to redeem our history. Cosmic praise and a call: for Christ to find at last this "world summit [which he needs] for his consummation" (Teilhard de Chardin).

Some eucharistic hymns: Pss. 33; 103; 113; 117; 145; cosmic hymns: Pss. 8; 19; 29; 104.

2. Actions of graces

The feature of these psalms is the joy, as in the hymns. But with this difference, God is celebrated in them on account of a particular benefit regarding the people or an individual (action of graces, collective or individual).

The **literary structure** often comprises three elements (e.g., Ps. 66):

(a) announcement that God will be praised;

(b) account of the peril faced (often in very general terms, as in the psalms of supplication) and of divine intervention; trust in God is referred to;

(c) an invitation to those assisting to participate in this action of graces.

The **doctrine:** this is the joy of experiencing personally or collectively God's faithfulness to his people and to each of those faithful to him. A feeling also that God's bounties should be "confessed" to bear witness to the nations.

Christian prayer: the action of graces (in Greek, "eucharistia") is so fundamental for a Christian that it has become the cult act pre-eminent. Marveling joy to receive oneself at every instant of our lives, as being saved and loved by the Father in his Son.

Some psalms: collective (Ps. 124); individual (Pss. 22; 32; 34; 66).

3. Psalms of supplication. Lamentations

The most numerous (one-third of the Psalter) and among the most baffling.

The **central theme:** an upright man describes with strength of feeling his illness or the persecutions he endures and asks God for deliverance. What kind of suffering is involved? Sometimes physical illness with multiple descriptions. Do not be put off by the hyperboles: for us an illness is described by the days in the hospital; at this period (and in how many countries still!) an illness meant the prospect of the shadow of death. More profoundly, it is often a matter of moral suffering translated into physical terms, the suffering of a man who has abandoned his "will-to-live," who is bowed down enough to die. For the Semite, all inner suffering is translated by physical hurt (even we have heartache over suffering). Last, this suffering is persecution still. One has the impression that this upright man is persecuted because he suffers. In the mentality of the time (remember Job), a sick man was a sinful man (a very deep-rooted idea in the human mind: to find the cause of people's misfortune).

The **literary structure** is not strict. Diverse elements may be found (for the sake of example we are taking Ps. 22):

(a) invocation to God. Often the name of God uttered like a cry suffices;

(b) lament in which the sufferer explains his wretchedness (Ps. 22:7-19);

(c) supplication. Relations between God and his faithful one are direct and trusting. "Lord, come quickly to my help" (Ps. 22:20-22);

(d) motifs on which the faithful builds his trust. The supplication relies on qualities of God (tenderness, love, faithfulness) and man's religious attitude: his faith, his certainty of being rescued (Ps. 22:4-6, 10-12, and passim);

(e) action of graces on occasion at the close of these prayers, so sure is the faithful one of being rescued (Ps. 22:23-27).[6]

The **doctrine** is the mystery of suffering. A "mystery" meaning a situation within which I am, thus with no possibility of drawing back in order to "understand"; one thing for which there is thus no explanation, and this is why the wretched man cries out as the situation "bites." The cry of Ps. 22 in human terms is a desperate one, "My God, my God, why have you deserted me?"

But his suffering, which was personal to him, gradually takes on a "prophetic" aspect; it becomes the symbol of universal suffering; the unfortunate man becomes the figure of all sufferers and all the persecuted from Abel the virtuous man, Moses, Jeremiah, etc. Liturgical utilization of these individual prayers must have helped this development to take place. The cry of **one** who suffers becomes the cry of **all those** who come to ask God for succor and thank him. It thus becomes a fit medium for the cry of all those who will suffer to the world's end.

In the meantime, by means of the poems of the Suffering Servant, in Isaiah (see p. 114), one begins to understand that this suffering—which is incomprehensible—can have a meaning: it can be redeeming. From this ordeal (for it remains an ordeal) of suffering, God can cause salvation to spring. Ps. 22:28-32 witnesses this interpretation, this deepening of the meaning: the poor man who suffered is become **the** poor man of all time; his salvation is greeted as the symbol of messianic salvation: all mankind that is saved gathers together to sing the praises of God the Savior.

Christian prayer: Jesus presents himself and utters these plain, world-shaking words, "I am that poor man." On the Cross, he dies, crying, "My God, my God, why have you deserted me?" Jesus partakes of our suffering; he puts himself in the ranks of all those who suffer and want to know why. In suffering and in dying, Jesus is doing nothing new; he is content to be a poor man, one of the poor men of all time. And so this cry he utters on the Cross is the cry of his own suffering, but it is the immense cry of all unfortunate men. This unique cry on the Cross thus echoes and re-echoes to the ends of the earth, carried by the chorus of all unfortunates whose voice is this psalm. Our suffering now can no longer be thought of outside of Christ on the Cross. Our suffering, and that of all our brethren that we carry in our prayer, puts us in the immense orchestra of the psalms of suppli-

cation. The meaning of this tragic symphony, the song of
the soloist renders it: our suffering, and all our rebellion,
passing through the mouth of the Son of God, become a
prayer, redeeming for our brethren and for us.

Some psalms: 22; 25; 38; 51 (**Miserere**); 130 (**De pro-
fundis**).

4. The wisdom psalms

Reflective themes dear to the saints. Three subjects
warrant further mention.

(a) Cult of saints

Compare two psalms that are closely parallel: 111 and
112. Extraordinary substitution in a people who so strongly
held the feeling of God's transcendence: Ps. 112 simply
applies to the virtuous man what Ps. 111 said of God!
This is the biblical foundation of the cult of saints and
divinization of the Christian as taught us by Paul and
John in their time.

Christian prayer: Ps. 112 begins with a word which has
its importance: the Protestants tend to keep it only, the
Catholics to forget it only. "Allelu-Yah!" Praise be to God.
The cult of saints is a praise to God, never to the saints,
to God who sets a gleam of his saintliness shining in this
or that saint; praise to God who is the total saintliness of
the Father present among us. And all the saints only re-
produce one aspect. It is God who is praised in them.

May we never forget: it is not so much a question of
praying St. Thérèse but the God of St. Thérèse, meaning,
God better known for having made St. Thérèse shine
palely reflecting his splendor (the orisons of the Mass are
our model in this domain).

A note on the psalms of the "Pharisee." The danger of the kind of thing lay in going from "Happy is the man who," etc. to "Happy am I who," etc. And the priest at Mass every day must declare, **Lavabo inter innocentes,** I am among the saints, etc.

There seem to me to be two ways of saying these psalms.

First, with **simplicity.** To make wondering contemplation of God's work in me. "The Lord has done wonders for me," etc. Man is "creature," meaning God's master-work; at times there is a good deal of vanity and shamelessness in calling oneself "nothing" (does it not mean telling God, "Lord your masterwork is . . . junk"!). Man's real feeling before his Maker is expressed in Ps. 139:14:

> For all this, O God, I thank you
> for the wonder of myself.

Second, with **humility,** since I am well aware—and this is where the talk of "nothing" comes in—of being far from having let God realize in me the dream of saintliness he had about me. Gap between my life and God's dream (my "vocation") that I express in these psalms. Gulf in Christ on the Cross: in the same being coexisted the saintliness of God and the sinfulness he took on for our sakes, the terrible gulf of his death on the Cross and our redemption. Christian, I am "saint" and always sinner. The humble recognition of this discrepancy (which becomes an abyss in moments of lucidity and in some saints), calling on God's all-powerful bountifulness, united with the suffering of the one who was crucified, can also be redemptive.

Some psalms: 1; 26; 112.

(b) Cult of law

The attitude of Saul the Pharisee before the road to Damascus could be summed up very briefly as "my life is the law." God's law given by Moses on Sinai was the concretization of the covenant, this dialogue of "I" and "Thou" between God and his people (singular), this dialogue creating the people as one People. The people never ceased from meditating on this and finding the way ahead thereby. From the time of exile, this assiduous frequenting will begin to become a real cult. This cult will verge at times on superstition. Nonetheless there is something admirable in this passionate love of the Pharisee for the law. The historian Josephus (a contemporary of Christ) wrote, "It is natural for all Jews from their birth to think the divine will is in all of them [laws], to respect them and if need be die for them with joy."

Something special will be said only of the most famous of them all, Ps. 119, with its litany of 176 invocations.

Ps. 119: intimacy in prayer with God who is "All-other" and yet "near" us through his Word.

Eight synonyms for the word "law" occurring in each of the eight-line stanzas of these twenty-two strophes; each stanza beginning with the twenty-two letters of the alphabet in sequence: composing this rhythmically compelling incantation. It is not a meditation on the law, however, but a dialogue with God, the prayer of someone who has met God, who felt called upon by him and required to respond. "The psalmist speaks to God and if he dares, it is because God spoke to him first. His prayer is a response to God's call, a call which is not only inward but is also this divine Word contained in the holy books. By this Word, God unceasingly invites the Israelites to the dialogue of prayer" (M. F. Lacan). And the fruit of the dialogue (see vs. 151), the murmured, rapt, "Yahweh, you are closer still."

Christian prayer. The convert Paul had only this to say, "My life is the Christ." We know that this law, this word God addressed to his people in the Old Testament, he addresses to us in the living Word made flesh. What we have to do is go through this whole psalm replacing the word "law" and its synonyms by the reality they represent: Jesus. And "while we repeat Psalm 119 contemplating Jesus, Word of the Father, and joining in his filial praise with him, God will let us taste the inner presence of his Son, in whom he has told us and given us everything, and our Lord will let us see the face of his Father" (M. F. Lacan).

Some psalms: 19; 119.

(c) Problem of retribution

"If you do good, you will be rewarded; if you do evil, punished"; this general principle is stated with force in Deuteronomy and there is no answer to it—except that the facts do not bear it out. For, not knowing the other world, equilibrium was expected in this one. For a long while, this problem was veiled by consciousness of solidarity. In the face of misfortune or ill-health (meaning God's punishment) of an innocent party, it was always possible to reassure the victim thus, "It's the king's fault or else your grandfather's," etc. (the dead had broad shoulders!).

As the exile approached, God wanted to lay stress on **individual** responsibility. It was vital to stop the Jews' despairing. Exile was going to destroy the people as Special People: in the frame of reference of overstrict belief in solidarity, each individual would have had to recognize himself as irremediably rejected of God, since the people were so. Jeremiah and then Ezekiel declare, "There will be no more saying, The fathers have eaten unripe grapes and the children's teeth are set on edge; each man will die for his own sinning." Personal hope became possible. But the problem of retribution had been stated.

Some twenty psalms mark the move to a solution which will only appear in the New Testament. Four stages may be distinguished:

(1) **Calm in the face of the problem** (e.g., Ps. 128).

It is enough to restate traditional doctrine.

Provided the terms are transposed to celestial reward of the Spirit, these psalms perfectly express our hope for reward in the next world.

(2) **Amazed suffering** (e.g., Pss. 10; 94).

"If there were a good God, would he let his children die?" One is aware of the problem. One does not know how to reply. Saddened or impassioned call to divine providence for all to be restored to order.

God is not angry with us if on some days this is what we pray (he has inspired and had these psalms preserved for them to be ours, unashamedly). In any case, the "prayer" of many men. May it cast a ripple on the still waters of our Christian assurance, a bit too sure of having an answer to everything and living in peace while the world suffers!

(3) **Peace in faith** (e.g., Pss. 91; 139)

The value of the prosperity of the wicked is denied and the stress laid on the true well-being of the virtuous:

God's protection will certainly triumph over present crises. Faith that is merit-worthy, but hope for temporal restoration.

(4) Joy in love (e.g., Ps. 73)

This Ps. 73 is a high point of the Old Testament. After affirming naked faith ("You are good—No, cries my blood," Marie Noël's cry), the psalmist reviews his ordeal: tempted by the prosperity of the wicked, by the effectiveness of methods he ought to reprove, he begins to doubt. "Why should I keep my own heart pure, and wash my hands in innocence?" He suffers, and submits because he serves God. Death stares him in the face, definitive ordeal (more so for him than for us who await resurrection). And suddenly because God's love is on him, he murmurs, "I do not know what will happen next, but I love you too much not to continue to love you, "My happiness lies in being close to you; in the end, you will receive me into glory."

"God's aim is achieved: all the preparations of the centuries led to this: [the outrage of suffering and death] surmounted by awareness of existential plentude, extraordinarily valid and source of the greatest joy, in the response itself of man faithful to the faithfulness of God" (E. Rideau).

5. Psalms of malediction, psalms of consecration

"Lord kill them all. Those who conspire against me, break them in the teeth"; "May the upright man bathe his feet in the blood of the wicked."

This kind of "prayer" is found throughout the Psalter. Out of date? Have you noticed that many of these psalms occur in liturgy, especially in Holy Week? The Church felt they were the most suitable to let us into the heart of

Christ offering himself upon the Cross for the forgiveness of his enemies. Paradox? Not really; let us consider together a biblical theme, that of the avenger.

The "divine avenger" of Isaiah is one of the most terrible texts of the Old Testament. Read it through, first: Isa. 63:1-6 (clarified by Isa. 59:15-20).

God takes vengeance on the enemies of Israel, all symbolized by Edom (an enemy people from across the Dead Sea). Thus God saves his people. One gets the impression the prophet rejoiced. One is, however, rather uneasy before this avenger coming from the wine-press where he has crushed his enemies, his clothes and feet dripping their blood.

One tries to understand; these enemies for the psalmist in the year 500 B.C. had a concrete face and form: Edom, and all the rest. For the Holy Spirit who inspired these words, what was their face and form? Who could think of Jesus praying with these psalms? For whose destruction could he ask except for the one for whom it was impossible for him to pray, namely the "world." "I am not praying for the world" (John 17:9, in the priestly prayer expressing the feelings Christ had in his heart when giving his life for us!). The "world" of St. John, meaning the Evil One, with all its manifestations in our world: harm, suffering, sin, death, everything that is refusal of God, turned back on itself. One begins to sense that we may be something quite else than spectators in this terrible fight, that this blood which is shed could well be . . . but why go on imagining when John himself has undertaken to explain it to us.

Revelation (19:11-21). John tells us clearly, the Avenger is Christ leading the definitive battle against the beasts,

symbols of evil and the Evil One. But then Edom and
the historical nations of Isa. 63 were already images of
these beasts,[7] of these powers of evil against whom Christ
leads a fight to the death: objectively, Satan, but also
subjectively all the works of Satan in us, our sins, our backsliding, our connivance with evil. Both evil and evil-in-us!
Thus we are no longer spectators thirsting for the blood
of our enemies. For this battle is taking place everywhere
there is sin to destroy: first in the carnal body of Christ
on whom God laid the burden of our sins ("For our sake
God made him into sin," 2 Cor. 5:21) and also in each
one of us. And this battle then becomes dramatic to the
highest degree: this blood which is shed, it is that of Christ,
it is that of the sinner, it is our own blood.[8]

Psalms of consecration: without paradox, may it not be
said that these psalms of malediction are in their plenary
literal meaning psalms of consecration, and that they are
perhaps among the prayers which carry us the furthest
and most personally into the mystery of the redemption:
we ask God to grant that he measure us upon the cross
and cut away whatever is excessive. "Father," prayed
Father Lyonnet "do with me as you will—here I am: work
in me, measure and cut away." "Lord, here I am before
you defenseless, so to say; I offer myself to your tempering
blows. Destroy all which is bad in me, all which is refusal
of you and keeps me from being united with your Son."

How—when the Lord grants us the grace of being
present in the words we utter—can we recite them from
the bottom of the heart without feeling the secret fear
lest he take us at our word?

6. Psalms of pilgrimage, to Jerusalem and the temple

Here I group together psalms of various families which

have this in common: they center in Jerusalem or Zion or the temple and—they get on our nerves. What is it to do with me, this temple destroyed nineteen centuries ago; how can I say in all seriousness,

> Jerusalem, if I forget you,
> may my right hand wither!
> Ps. 137:5-6

Yet these psalms are linked by the deepest religious spirit and fervor in the Bible, and through them we may enter it in prayer.

Nearing the end of our study of the Old Testament, we appreciate how much the whole history of the revelation and of the people tends to the one end-purpose: tends to "The one who is coming," to the building of this Kingdom where God will be all things in all men, to the achievement of this total body of the Christ. We also know that it will not be reached except by the efforts of a whole people on the move together: this Kingdom, body of Christ, it is all made of God (he comes down from heaven) and all made of mankind (the achievement of our history). To hasten this coming by supplicating God to grant it and by all of us taking the road together: such is the object of these psalms of pilgrimage. The only thing is that instead of expressing it in abstract terms, they do it with an image, by the symbol of the temple.

Now what we must do is to study this theme as it appears throughout the Bible.

The theme of the temple, or the meaning of history under the form of symbol: God starts from a reality men know well, that is to say, the temple, the place God inhabits. In three stages he is going to reveal to us that this place where he wants to go and dwell is in the first instance a house of stone, but also a faithful people.

Stage 1.   The Old Testament.

God "really" inhabits his temple: the tent in the Wilderness to begin with, where he makes himself present to Moses on the propitiatory between the two cherubim, later the Jerusalem temple, the temple David wanted and Solomon built.

God dwells amidst his people and his people gather in this holy place to meet God together. Holy place, known by the names of temple, Zion, Jerusalem, etc.

Once this value is well established, God prepares for the next stage. The prophets yearn for a more intimate and more spiritual presence. Refer back for example to what Zephaniah said, God will live "in the midst of Jerusalem, meaning in the bosom of the daughter of Zion, the people in fact" (see p. 77, parallel between his message and the account of the Annunciation) or the marvelous description of the temple-to-be given by Ezekiel.

Stage 2.   Jesus declares that the real temple, the place where God dwells and where men are met together, is the "sanctuary that was his body" (John 2:21). His carnal body for thirty-three years, living on amongst us to the world's end in the form of his eucharistic body.

But Christ's role is to "take unto himself" all men that they may become his enduring body. This brings us to the last stage.

Stage 3.   Paul and John in expounding the teaching of Jesus tell us that the real temple is surely to be found behind us and amongst us (Jesus carnal and eucharistic), but above all, before us; the mystic body it is our mission to build.

The gain will be appreciated, in approaching the mystic body as the fulfillment of the theme of the temple. Of all the explanations it has been possible to give us about this body, the impression no doubt remains as of something "unreal," nebulous and mystical. The Bible tells us that it is a temple. Now a temple is (1) solid, not an idea but stones. Stones, which is what Christians are, the living stones of St. Peter (see 1 Pet. 2:5); (2) where God lives. God also really lives (and it will be his definitive presence) in this body formed of all Christians at one with Jesus in this eucharistic body (have I the same respect for my brother—in whom God is present mystically —as for the Eucharist?); (3) a temple exists because **someone has built it.** God builds it, but in measure as Mary (a maiden from amongst us, of our race) has given Jesus his body, in measure as we Christians work for God to be really in us and in all things. Am I aware that communion with the eucharistic body is only a means for the building of his mystic body? Communion with Christ leads us inexorably to Catholic action.

"Jerusalem, if I forget you."

How could we ever forget? This impassioned love of the psalmist for the temple, for Zion, that is what our hearts hold dearest, impassioned love for the true temple which is the eucharistic body of Christ Jesus. "A single day in your courts [meaning, in intimacy with Christ] is worth more than a thousand elsewhere" (Ps. 84:10). Ardent desire for the House of God at last to be achieved, for Christ to attain "his perfect stature." The possessing Christ which is ours since the first Christmas and the Last Supper only quickens our desire for the final Coming—and this also depends on our apostolic action—in his definitive body.

"Amen; come, Lord Jesus" (Rev. 22:20).

Some psalms of pilgrimage: 27; 42-43 (psalm of "prayers at the foot of the altar" in the Mass); 63; 84; 122.

Note: the psalter as "affective dimension" of the Mass.

The Mass is liturgical action. Action, so it must go forward, it must move; liturgical, performed in common. In a half-hour!

There are occasions when one would like to stop and join onself in the consecration with the Lord Jesus, consecrating himself to the Father, in order to tell him in communion how much he is "our only expectation here below"; or stop at the Offertory to give explicitly the whole of its human dimension to the Host we are to consecrate: all our concrete life and that of our brothers for whom we are responsible, and so on. But it is liturgical action, the next man may not wish to pause at the same point as we do. In a half-hour!

Happily, throughout the day the Breviary for priests and those in religious orders, the Psalter for everyone when we so wish, by causing us to say over the psalms, permits us to take up the Mass again and pause to ponder this or that feeling that we have experienced therein. The psalms can carry our Mass throughout the day, throughout our lives.

In guidance:

At the foot of the altar	Pilgrimage
Confiteor	Lamentation
Liturgy of the Word	Psalm of the law
Offertory	Supplications
Lavabo	Psalm of the Pharisee
Preface	Hymns
Consecration	Maledictions
Pater	All! Royal psalms, etc.
Communion	Action graces. Cult of saints
Ite missa est	Pilgrimage to the mystic body

[1]A question of method, how to study the book of Psalms? I hope it is clear enough now that the first commentary on a biblical text is to fill in the background against which it took shape. That means dealing separately with each psalm—a hard task, as the divergent results testify.

In this chapter, for the sake of simplifying matters, I do not dwell on the dating. After indicating the three attitudes which seem to me to be fundamental, I shall be grouping the psalms by literary genre, with a few remarks on each of them.

[2]Refer back to what was said about David, p. 50.

[3]There is a difference of one number between the order in the Hebrew text and the Greek followed by the Vulgate and the liturgy. Recent translations (like the Jerusalem Bible) follow the Hebrew system, and this is used here (not that of the liturgy which you·will find in your Office of the Mass).

What it amounts to is that the Latin is one number behind the Hebrew.

[4]A choice has to be made here also and I gladly recommend to your attention two books. One is synthesizing: P. Drijvers, *Les Psaumes, genres littéraires et thèmes doctrinaux* (Cerf, 1958); Eng. trans.: *The Psalms* (Herder Book Center). The other is more analytical: A. George, *Prier les psaumes* ("The psalms for prayer") in the series "Equipes enseignantes," 1960.

[5]Of the hymns, the royal psalms afford an interesting comparison. Some celebrate the king of Israel (e.g., Pss. 2; 110). The king as "lieu-tenant" of God held an exceptional position

in the nation. It is not therefore out of the way that in celebrating God's handiwork, the one by whom it is carried out should have a special place of honor.

Pss. 2 and 110, celebrating the enthronement of the king, will naturally sing in the New Testament of the true king of Israel, Jesus, enthroned in his office of judge by his resurrection and exaltation.

Others celebrate Yahweh the king (e.g., Pss. 93-100).

During the exile, when there was no earthly king any longer, God came to be sung—especially in Second Isaiah—as the only king of Israel, the manifestation of whose glorious and definitive Kingdom lay in the awaited future.

Christian prayer takes them as an amplification of *Pater*, "may your Kingdom come."

[6]Verses 28-32 are, without doubt, relics of a "re-reading" of the psalm. A prayer we said as children sometimes takes on deeper meaning after years of experience and suffering. This is what happened with these prayers, incessantly repeated age after age: each generation set down the best of the understanding that it got.

[7]Plenary meaning can be spoken of here, since John takes up the same Old Testament words to reveal to us the hidden reality. See above, p. 24.

[8]The Church in the liturgy for Good Friday makes explicit the same idea. As the second reading in the Mass, we have the fourth Song of the Suffering Servant (Isa. 53), namely, the most clear text on expiatory suffering. It is then enough to string together the three lessons—the Avenger, the Suffering Servant, and the Passion according to St. Luke—to understand that the "wine-press of his wrath is also the wine-press of sufferings. The one who tramples is also the one who is trampled. This is the mystery of the wine-press. Christ, the Son of God, the presser; Christ Son of man, the grape that is pressed!" (Ae. Loehr). The orison before the second lesson tells it with tragic brevity: the blood is that of Christ on the Cross; for him, death, and for us, resurrection.

VIII.

THE VIRGIN ISRAEL IS GOING TO BEAR A SON, AND HE SHALL BE CALLED "GOD-SAVES": JESUS

Marxist meaning of history. Biblical meaning of history.

The Marxist of today, like the man of the Bible, feels himself embarked on history with a meaning, the whole tending to the paradise where "there will be no more death, and no more mourning or sadness" (Rev. 21:4). The one and the other know that this paradise will be the fruit of human endeavor on the part of a whole people working together.

The only thing, to use the symbolic language of the Bible, is that the Marxist turns himself into a man working with might and main for something which of itself remains purely human, and which requires his initiative alone to obtain.

The biblical man knows that he stands before God like a woman bringing to birth with all her love that which is the common work of God and man.

We have often referred to this nuptial aspect, which God wanted to give his covenant with man. On the very threshold of the New Testament, it is an appropriate time to treat of this marriage as a whole.

God's covenant with man in the image of human marriage

God wanted not only to be the Father of humanity in giving them all in life by his creation. He wanted to call man to join him in the creation by free acceptance of God's gift. Of this, God found no better symbol than the mutual fulfillment of man and wife in marriage.

Refer back to the second account of the creation, where Adam so sorrowfully expresses his "incompleteness" on being alone, and the theological commentary provided in the first account (Gen. 1:27): this certainty has never been more strongly expressed, that man and woman are not fulfilled (and are not "God's image") except in their mutual gift of love.

But this mutual gift, which is their fulfillment and requires their whole activity, man and wife accomplish each according to his own vocation inscribed in the flesh as in the heart.

Man is, first, the one who gives, who makes fruitful. His activity is, first, of initiative. He is the one who starts the game.

Woman is, first, the welcoming one, receptiveness. In this gift of herself which is the welcoming, she becomes fruitful.

This is why, when marriage will appear as the symbol of activity in common between God and humanity, God, whose initiative remains his and incommunicable, will always be represented by man; humanity, whose task is to let God lead, will always be represented by a female figure: the daughter of Zion, Jersualem, the virgin Israel, then Mary and the Church.[1]

Marriage begins to appear as the symbol with the prophet Hosea. In his time, it was 1,000 years since God had made the covenant with his people (still to be born) in the person of Abraham; it was 500 years since the contract became effective by means of Moses on Mount Sinai. From then on, God and his people are bound by a bilateral arrangement, outside of which Israel would not be able to live. Hosea was chosen by God to reveal to the people that this bond is a love-bond. You remember how, in the marriage which was Hosea's experience, his love was so strong it gave back to his unfaithful wife her virginity of heart.

This was in advance the history of the people and of each one of us in that people. Purified by the suffering of the captivity, the people of God, like an erring promised bride, became once again the beloved virgin in the eyes of God. God then subjected her to a test of faithfulness by the painful education of her faith, hope, and love by means of the persecution and in the midst of the temptation of Hellenist humanism (see p. 156). A little Remnant of the people were faithful to God. And with them we arrive at the dawn of the New Testament. This people of "poor men," utterly abandoning themselves in the arms of God, await with all their being the Savior, the Messiah. For God answered his people's Prayer of "Ah, if the heavens would only open and you come down!" with "The daughter of Zion is going to bear the new prophet."

The poor people wait, they hope, and they go on praying.

Then God, like a bridegroom-to-be, tries to evoke with infinite respect the beloved's response; God is going to evoke from his people the loving response which will enable him to be born of them.

The virgin Israel bows her head, "Be it done with me according to your word."

To the space-time coordinates, the Virgin Mary—because she is one of the "poor people"—is the voice of this whole people, welcoming in love and in her bosom "God the Savior" (in Hebrew, "Yo-Shuah," or Jesus). Mary—gratuitously and without any merit on her part—chosen in love by God's Son, becoming by acceptance the bride of the Word before she is his Mother.

The threefold aspiration inscribed in the depths of created being is thus miraculously brought to pass. Mary is the **bride:** this harmony of the couple, sign of the completeness each receives at the hands of the other, Mary knows by her response to God's love, for he chooses her before all women. This intimate union is formed, first of all, in Mary's heart: "She conceived in her heart [faith] before she conceived in her womb," as St. Leo put it. Intimacy without parallel between God and his creature, the very same we shall know in heaven. Mary is the **virgin:** this nostalgia after purity, after total giving with no holding back, felt by every man in the depths of his being, is realized in Mary. To make this virginity of heart appear to our sight, God wanted that in Mary it should transfigure her very flesh. This physiological and psychological blossoming of the young bride, she will receive uniquely from her intimacy with the Son of God. Mary is the **mother:** the aspiration to fecundity, to carry on one's own being into another, is brought to pass in Mary beyond all the bounds of hope; with one and the same love, she loves God and her Son.

Joyous nativity in Bethlehem.

Sorrowing nativity at Calvary. It is only there that

this three-fold aspiration of humanity will be accomplished for all time; there God and humanity give themselves to one another forever in virginity. The Son of God who during his lifetime presented himself as the Bridegroom (Matt. 9:15; John 3:25-30), upon the Cross gives himself to us: unique act rendered present down the ages in the sacraments, calling for love from each of us. The people of God, the new Church, is there at the foot of the Cross, wholly summed up in Mary. In her, this people accept the sorrowful gift of their salvation and fruitfulness: unique assent within which each of our acceptances down the ages will find room.

For what was accomplished once and for all on Calvary? The gift from God in his Son, acceptance on the part of the Church in Mary, are only the beginning of this life of intimacy between God and his people, between God and every one of us. The fruit should be Christ achieved, this total Christ having attained his full stature, in whom we shall all be met together for everlasting life without sorrowing and without death, in the eternal ecstasy of the ever-plenary and ever-new gift. That is the world's end which the book of Revelation reveals to us: the apostle John contemplates the marriage of the Lamb (Jesus, "God-saves"—but immolate, that is, eternally redeeming) and his bride, the Church got ready by God for the Bridegroom (Rev. 19:8). John sees the bride come down from heaven: this means that the state of love, eternally faithful because founded on the faithfulness of God, is not the result of our endeavors but, first, a gift of God's.

This communion with God which our eternal life will be is still the object of our attention. But this communion is already invisibly at work in each one of us.

It is also visibly present in our world by two "signs": the sacrament of marriage, the "sacrament" of virginity consecrated to God.

Marriage has already been referred to (see p. 150). This is the source of the spirituality of married Christians: by loving one another, they are the sign for the rest of us carnal beings who must see in order to understand, of the ever-young tenderness of God for us, and our response; they are the "sacrament," the effective sign of this same tenderness, meaning that, by loving one another, they make humanity love God a mite more. "This sacrament is a great one," St. Paul says, "in it I see the union of Christ and his Church" (cf. Eph. 5:25-32). For as long as our carnal world shall endure, there is nothing therefore finer than marriage.

But when the world's end comes and heaven reigns over all, we shall no longer be in need of proceeding by a sign, however fine, to taste and understand God's love. In heaven, there will be no more Eucharist, this sign that makes Jesus Christ present among us, since we shall be forever united with him and will see him "as he sees us." In heaven, we shall no longer have to proceed by the sign of marriage in order to understand the tenderness of God. We shall, each of us and all as one, be totally and definitively united with Christ in the most unimaginable intimacy of all. Concerning this intimacy—Christ calls certain men and certain women to live it here below by asking them to "consecrate themselves" to him, to live on the earth for him alone (and thus for the other people who are already his body). In heaven, there will be only virginity.

Marriage and virginity: two "vocations," each as fine as the other in its respective order, terrestrial or celestial.

The order of virginity is only superior because it already belongs to the new world.

And the two need each other. Those who have consecrated to the Lord their virginity need to feel the tenderness of married couples near them: it constitutes for them a constantly renewed call to love Christ and their brethren with one and the same tenderness. Married people need to "see" the end-point of their loving near them: their mutual love should be leading them together to love each other and love God as profoundly as priests and nuns love God.

Married people, people consecrated to God: God has called us (our "vocation") to give, together, in our world an image of his love. This love is so rich and plenary that God has had to make us "specialize" here below in this role of signs. But he also wanted both kinds to find themselves in Mary, who is in advance the image of the Church of heaven, the model and the perfecting to the full of our vocations.

This introduction to the Bible could not end better than by contemplating Mary. She stands in effect at the summit of time.

Mary at one moment of time was the people of God poorly welcoming the Lord; she in whom the whole Old Testament is replete, the little girl born of a people she entirely sums up in herself, she in whom all those who await salvation see themselves.

But in her there is also present the whole New Testament. Mary the first of the redeemed, the mother of God's Son and of all God's sons, at the foot of the Cross was God's new people accepting, sorrowing, the gift of her

Lord. Mary figures for the Church. All our Christian life, which is personal acceptance of Christ, can only be lived within the Yes uttered once and for all time on Calvary. All our life is Marian.

Little, or nothing, has been said of her in these pages. Yet she is everywhere, and in her true place. With all tradition, we give Mary a place unique in our history. But—and the theme of marriage helps us understand this— always on the side of the creature, the created being. We say once again and strongly how far we are in agreement with our Protestant brothers in reproving some excesses of false Marian piety that might make it be believed that we as Catholics put her on the same plane as Christ. Mary is a **creature** as we are, **redeemed** like us and more than us, since God redeemed us from sin but kept her pure from sin, the first of the redeemed, by grace. But among created beings, she has a place that is unique at the side of Christ. As a believer, she is like us in the Church. Insofar as she is the figure of the Church, she remains the one in whom the Word was made flesh, also the one in whom each of us, wrapped in her virginal love, responds with her in saying Yes to Christ; she, lastly, is the one who stands before our eyes, the figure of that Church at the world's end, the Kingdom of God that we are building, the anticipated image of the coming to pass of God's plan, which is the end-point of our history.

[1]You understand there is no misogyny in the place man seems to hold in the Bible. Man is God's symbol, woman is humanity's (men and women). This is also the reason, no doubt, why the Church cannot accept women as priests. The priests carry on Christ's mission, which is God, in respect of humanity.

CONCLUSION:

PRESENT-DAY VALUE OF
THE OLD TESTAMENT

"The Old Testament . . . I do not understand any of it. Besides, what is the good reading it nowadays when we have Christ?"

Objection heard a hundred times. Ought this book to have begun with refuting that charge? Why should I not have left you the joy of doing that for yourselves? The few pages that now follow will teach you nothing; they are only intended to help you in expressing what our reading will have already made you appreciate: the Old Testament—the Old-age Testament as Pascal and M. Pouget put it—is young.

"The Old Testament . . . I understand none of it"

To tell you the truth, the one who doesn't understand is me! There has never been a time (I am speaking for the Western world) when its language was so in tune as it is with ours. After a millennium and more of the civilization of the book, with the advent of cinema and television, we have entered the civilization of the image. "The cinema . . . I simply don't understand it!" None of you would dare say that because it is not true: the cinema "speaks" to us, the image has its own language and sometimes we catch on to it without the help of concept in between. On the screen, all is symbol: every image, every movement of the camera means to say "something else," and we find no difficulty in sensing behind the "universe of forms" the message coming across to us.

The Bible is less of a book than a film; it is the family picture album of God. Perhaps we understand nothing because we want to be "reading" it, when it would be enough just to be "looking" at it. It puts us out because on opening it we expect it to tell us about God in the hard-and-fast language of our philosophy textbooks or our catechism. It does not speak of the Church but shows us a living people, loving and sinning, a "promised bride" beloved and unfaithful; it does not define the mystic body but raises before our eyes the temple (which is us) where God dwells; it does not teach us to recite **acts** (!) of contrition or humility but invites us to be the prodigal son and the baby safe-and-sound in his mother's arms.

Not a book but a door, the door to the "biblical universe" in which we live. It is one of the graces of getting to know it that it gives us a picture of the whole world, all that is human, all that is cosmos, "fraternal" and "sacramental." One is amazed on putting it down to discover that suddenly everything speaks of God to us: the little brother one hugs to oneself (that is how God loves me and how I must let myself be loved by him), the tenderness of the engaged couple, like the human effort and the suffering of the world, nature (see Ps. 104) and the heavenly bodies (the moon faithful to her course ought to make us think of the faithfulness of God, see Pss. 89; 38). It is the Bible's grace to be the exorcising of our world. Everything in our world that spelled temptation becomes to us a call to love God. Temptation of impurity, of trifling: call to respect human love, the finest image of God's love. Temptation of the technological, to believe only in the earthly: call to build the total body of Christ. The earth? "All of its sorcery leaves me unharmed since it became for me, through itself, the body of the one who is and the one to come!" (Teilhard de Chardin).

In a language which has become our own again,[1] the Bible tells us of Christ: the Old Testament aids us in understanding the Christ; it makes us enter into a people on the move toward Christ, the end-point of our history.

1. The Old Testament helps us to understand the historical Christ

Blaze of white light. To have revealed to me the unified splendor of the heavens, I need these two horizons stretching it out like a bow and bearing in its purified atmosphere which serves as a prism, the sevenfold beauty.

Blaze of God's glory on the face of Christ. Like Paul on the road to Damascus, blinded by the dazzling light, I need the prism of the two Testaments which serve to difract its multiple splendor for me across a thousand years of reflection and two thousand years of history.

Clearly there can be no question of going over all the roads, here and now, that lead through Old Testament country to.Christ.[2] Let us stop a while at two of them only.

(A) The Old Testament helps us to understand the being of Christ.

Christ: for the philosopher, the paradox of being. At the meeting of two worlds, coexistence of the finite and the infinite, of the one and the multiple, of God and creature.

The Old Testament does not make us understand the mystery of Christ. It aids us to get a grasp on all aspects, placing him at the point where the two roads of reflection converge (this summarizes what was said at the start of the chapter on wisdom, p. 135).

Wisdom at the start was commonsense, straightforward and simple; it will always be felt as belonging to us, what we have that is best; to make us understand Christ, the Wisdom of God, is thus at the climax of what is best of ourselves.

The Word of God, on the contrary, reaches us with all the mystery of its transcendence; calling Christ the Word is to remind ourselves constantly of his mystery and the transcendence of "All-other."

Paradox for the philosopher: Christ is one for each man involved in history. He is the synthesis of their contradictory desires: I await salvation but I want to be the author, I want to be saved by man. And yet I know full well that I can only be saved by God, etc.

(B) The Old Testament aids us in understanding how Christ will exercise his mission as Savior.

A man like us, Jesus the "son of David."

Read the Gospel, and you will find this is one of the titles most frequently given Jesus by his audience. Note the care with which Matthew and Luke establish (following the criteria of the period, very different from our own) his genealogy. And Jesus himself accepts the title. That was important: the title witnessed that he was indeed of our race, one of us, that he—like ourselves—had a long line of forebears, saint and sinner.

So Jesus accepts the title. But he rejects the content which the Jews gave the title. Each time it is attributed to him, he answers, "Yes, I am . . . the servant who suffers" or the "Son of man."

The point was that in recognizing his manhood, his contemporaries risked forgetting the other aspects of his personality.

A man who saves us by his suffering: Jesus, the servant.

"The offspring of your body," God told David, "will be a son to me, and I shall be a father to him. I will make his royal throne secure for ever" (cf. 2 Sam. 7). The covenant was thus "regalized" (Gelin): the son of God was not so much "Israel" as "Israel-summed-up-in-their-king." The hope for a brighter future henceforth was thus to find a practical outlet in awaiting the world's end when a son of David's will be temporal king and establish definitively God's Kingdom upon earth.

Isaiah attempted in God's name to spiritualize this hope: at the birth of Hezekiah, he had described the future work of the king in terms so extraordinary that Israel ought to have understood it was a spiritual Kingdom he was speaking of (Isa. 7; 9; 11). But the people took these oracles literally. God then had to resort to large-scale means: destroying those who would not give it up. Exile and the downfall of the Davidic dynasty. A disciple of Isaiah's then tries to draw the moral: the descendant of David will indeed save the people and establish the Kingdom of God, but he will do it by his suffering and his death.

His message was to be soon forgotten. The expectation of a warrior-king messiah became even greater, as the aftermath of the captivity was politically lamentable. It was such a son of David who was expected in the time of Christ.

"Yes, I am king," Jesus will say on his way to the Cross, "but my kingdom is not of this world" (John 18:36).

Jesus, man like us, saves us by taking on himself the burden of our suffering.

But Jesus is also All-other than us.

It is God alone who saves us: Jesus, Son of man.

Alongside this expectation of a messiah, man and king, another thread was announcing a Messiah coming from God.

Against the background of the persecution begun by Antiochus, the best of the Jews understand that salvation cannot come except from God. Daniel sees the wicked kingdoms destroyed by a "stone [meaning, the Messiah] breaking from the mountain untouched by hand" (Dan. 2:45); he develops this thought in chapter 7, showing us the Son of man "coming on the clouds of heaven."

This Son of man is going to hold an important place henceforth (and a mysterious one) in Jewish expectation. It is evidently not as yet suspected that this personage may be God, but he is transcendent, of the divine sphere and quasi-God. It was for having admitted this title that officially Jesus was condemned to death (Mark 14:62). Jesus certainly gave himself the title; it pleased him (perhaps because of the ambiguity: in current language, it signified only a man, and a humble man). And the theologian John, who lays such stress on salvation as a free gift, made it central to his Gospel. He had lived on close terms with the Lord, friend and friend, and to John it was evident he was man; yet he judged it important to stress the other aspect of his mystery: Jesus is God, the Son of man.

The Old Testament remains for us what it was for St. Paul, the "tutor to Christ." But it is not only the teaching master, it puts us on the move to Christ.

2. The Old Testament makes us one with a people on the move, on the move to Christ, who is the end-point of our history

Review of life in Catholic action: an hour spent thinking about one fact. The almoner reads a Gospel text and suddenly the text "speaks" to me. I had read it myself perhaps that very morning. It bored me or it seemed dull. But the text has not changed. What has changed is the fact that this evening I am expecting an answer.

Christ is born after 2,000 years of Bible history. Jesus is the end of the waiting of the whole Bible, moving forward sight unseen, in enthusiasm or in sin, toward the One who will save them.

The New Testament bores me, perhaps because I am no longer waiting. An answer which is not a response to something is no answer.

And that is the grace, once more, of the Old Testament, to make us take the road and get moving again. The grace of making every man who comes into contact with it aware that he too, perhaps unconsciously, tends toward something, toward someone. The Old Testament makes us discover—slowly, like a tutor and like a mother—that all our aspirations, all our disappointments, our need of love and purity, our unquenched thirst for justice, all this is a call to Someone. Meditating upon it, one cannot but feel part of a people on the move to some end. Whatever our sin, our faithlessness, our dissatisfaction, there will always be an Old Testament text to deal with it, to give us a welcome and set our feet back on the right road again. Grace of the Old Testament, so to take our lives— our poor lives—and give them a place in sacred history. In touch with this, one cannot but feel oneself part of a people passionately loved by God, by a God who counts on us for a welcome and for his birth in us and our brethren. The Church each year during Advent has us repeat this prayer of Isaiah: "Ah, if you would but rend heaven asunder and come down," etc. And he has come down, these two thousand years. But what we know about Christ, what he has already brought to pass, only makes the rest of the waiting the harder.

Christ is come. But not at our backs to drive us along like a flock of sheep. He is at the end-point of our history. We are impelled forward with our whole being, to the Christ of Parousia. This is the secret of joy and true dynamism.

The entire Old Testament culminates in the end-line of Revelation. St. John's prayer can but be our own:

"Amen; come, Lord Jesus."

[1]The language is the same. The principal difficulty lies, perhaps, in the fact that the Bible was born in a people of rural civilization. Certain symbols may need transposing to match our urban-industrial set-up.

[2]A valuable book has tried to achieve it: X. Léon-Dofour (ed.) *Vocabulaire de Théologie Biblique* (Cerf); Eng. trans.: *Dictionary of Biblical Theology* (Desclee, 1968).

INDEX OF THE BOOKS OF THE BIBLE